Dear ⌐

I hope you enjoy.

Georgie xxx.

SEMI-EDUCATED

This book is dedicated to all the wonderful teachers who have generously taught me so much. I miss our chats and the camaraderie in the staffroom. I am in awe of your dedication to your students, admire your devotion to the profession, and am envious of your skills in the classroom. I also hope you don't recognise anyone or anything, anywhere at all in this book.

Names and details have been obfuscated to protect the innocent. This book consists of things I may or may not have overheard and my own wildly exaggerated, half made-up and completely mistakenly remembered anecdotes from my time teaching. You know you can't trust a single thing I say.

SEMI-EDUCATED

Georgie Brooks

bad apple press

Semi-Educated

First published in 2022 in Australia and New Zealand by Bad Apple Press, Pty Ltd, ABN 62 630 105 065, Sydney and Perth.

22   8 7 6 5 4 3 2 1

ISBN: 9780645265149 eISBN: 9780645265156

 A catalogue record for this book is available from the National Library of Australia

Edited by Bad Apple Press
Editorial assistance by Teaspoon Consulting
Text typeset by Bad Apple Press
Cover design by Lisa Brewster
Proudly printed in Australia by Griffin Press, an Accredited ISO
AS/NZS 14001 Environmental Management System printer.

The paper used to produce this book is a natural, recyclable product made from wood grown in sustainable plantation forests. The manufacturing processes conform to the environmental regulations in the country of origin.

CONTENTS

1

A BIT OF SHUSH PLEASE

A noisy out-of-control classroom, packed with twenty-six teenagers simultaneously talking, laughing and shouting exudes a physical energy that can and does rattle windows. Their vitality could probably power all the electronic devices they have secreted on their person, in defiance of the school rules. As if I am in a dystopian novel, I can feel my life force being drained by the children surrounding me, who grow even more energised and powerful as I become weaker and unable to communicate at all.

'Quiet,' I say again, my voice rasping from trying to talk over their noise. Only the class good girl, in the first row in front of the teacher's desk, looks at me, but that seems to be out of pity rather than respect. Even she, I notice now, is openly drawing an artistic masterpiece (with a black Texta that I pray isn't a permanent marker) on her desk. Right where it will be visible to the Head of Middle School, who will be teaching a lesson in this classroom later in the day.

'A bit of shush, please,' I almost plead, terrified that the experienced teacher working in the next classroom will have to come and take control of my class. 'Stop that,' I snap to the boys who are rabbit punching the neck of a student in the row in front of them. Three girls cackle, with the maniacal laughter of the witches in Macbeth, and their victim bursts into tears and runs crying from the classroom. I know I should intervene, provide some pastoral care, but I'm unable to leave the rioting mob that are, in name only, under my control. Like all unruly hordes, they are terrifying. They exude the ominous scent of predators, an aroma of unchecked power, defiance and hormones.

'You will need to read chapter three and do the questions I handed out earlier for homework,' I say, and bravely turn to write this on the smeary whiteboard, scarily breaking eye contact and offering the class the opportunity to do something even worse than what they were doing while I was watching them. My announcement, along with nearly everything else I have said in this lesson, is ignored. My blood pressure is so high I am worried I will collapse with a heart attack in front of the class and I wonder, in the panicked reptilian part of my brain, almost the only section of my mind still functioning, whether the class will call for help or tear my body into pieces as a final manifestation of their power. There are still five minutes of the lesson to go, but most of the students have started slamming their books shut, zipping up pencil cases and standing up ready to go out and start their lunch break.

'The bell hasn't gone yet,' I bleat, in one final, futile attempt to impose my will on the class. I am sweating with nerves and shame, and stink of failure and desperation. No-one pays me any attention. The students start leaving, obeying some invisible primal urge, as if they are salmon heading upstream to spawn. At least no-one has spawned in my classroom. Or at least I hope not – I couldn't really see the back row of the class for the last half of the lesson.

Students walking briskly out of my classroom display more motivation, energy and purpose than they have shown in the preceding forty-five minutes. My classroom is deserted in seconds, with just discarded sweet wrappers and the photocopied homework questions lying crumpled on the desks, looking even more depressing under the white flickering fluorescent lights.

The posters on the classroom walls all sag and flap, like disappointed faces, revealing that some students have used my lesson to steal the drawing pins from the display boards again. No doubt the squeals I can hear echoing from the hallways are my students pricking each other with those pins. A large, laminated poster breaks completely free from the wall and slowly drifts towards me. I try to grasp it, but of course fail at this, as I have done with everything else this lesson. The poster is as slippery as a fish and I have to awkwardly jiggle and scrape at it to pick it up from the floor. It is a pastel peach colour, as synthetic as its inspirational statement, which proclaims in a nauseating font, 'If You Try, You Can Do Anything'. I can't even be bothered to try, or even remember why I wanted to try. I trudge off down the scuff-marked hallway after my students, to start my assigned yard duty, wandering all over the playground to stop any further bad behaviour, wondering hopefully whether I will pass a staff toilet on my way so I can do my first wee of the work day.

I don't know why I'm not sitting in a quiet office, about to go down for a coffee break with other civilised adults in a lovely inner-city café with a proper whistling coffee machine, gourmet food and no loud bells. I don't know why I ever thought I should do teaching and I really don't know if I'll ever actually be able to teach anyone anything. I'd wanted to help kids discover a love of learning and develop a life-changing passion for words and literature, but I've only enabled noise, chaos, mob rule and some children to get stabbed with drawing pins. The lunch bell finally rings, in a deafening discordant noise, from a speaker just above my head (at six foot tall I am not only closer to God, but closer to the noise). I jerk instinctively away from the painful sound and try to cover my ears, to the amusement of another group of teenagers (still seated in their class with their proper, in-control teacher), who are happily watching my antics through their classroom window. I try to pull myself up to my full height and assert some dignity. At least I haven't wet my pants, no mean achievement after having two four-kilo babies. Righto. Only yard duty and three lessons to go. Then it will be 3.30 and I can look forward to about six hours of marking and a panicked two hours of lesson prep for tomorrow. I don't think I will have any time spare to spend with my own children tonight.

The perfect work–life balance that I was deluded enough to think that teaching could offer is completely swung towards work and survival. Sleep and time with my family have been cast aside as I desperately try to keep pace with the demands of being a new teacher. Maslow's Hierarchy of Needs – something which we spent a lot of time on during my university-based training to be a teacher – sets out, in a neat pyramid, the needs that need to be met for all people before self-actualisation (and learning) can occur. At the bottom of the pyramid are the basic physiological needs for sleep and food. Although our focus was on the needs of the student, not of the teacher, I reflect dismally that I am not meeting even these. Hopefully tomorrow I can exert some control in the classroom and actually teach something, then go home, spend quality time with my family, catch up on my marking and lesson planning, and get to bed before midnight.

Everything is going just as I had hoped when I decided to become a teacher.

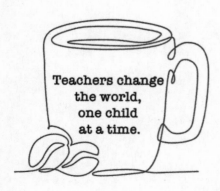
Teachers change the world, one child at a time.

2

OH MY GOD, THOSE HOLIDAYS

Everyone has an opinion about teachers and teaching. Correct that: everyone has a deeply held, highly subjective opinion about teachers and teaching that they want to share. Everyone has been taught by a teacher and, when they find out you are a teacher, everyone wants to tell you what their teachers were like. There are innumerable teachers depicted in literature, in films, in TV shows and in pop culture. Our society is saturated in teachers and with exploration of secondary school life. Maybe that is because for some (obviously terrible) people, secondary school was the high point of their life (imagine your fifteen-year-old personality being the best you could ever be). However, I think for most people it is because the combination of the trauma, the injustice and the missed opportunities of school haunt them forever. School is also twelve years of experience that you have in common with almost everyone else, giving a shared cultural reference point. Army veterans bond with their mates after serving just one six-month mission together, while at school you could potentially spend between six to twelve years in the same uniform, taking orders from the same people. The uncomfortableness of the uniform and the size of the gym might differ, but the school experience is pretty similar regardless of the school.

Everyone knows everything about teachers. They can tell you about their holidays (too long), their workdays (too short), the number of hours they spend with noisy children (too many), their whingeing (too much), their job (too easy), and their personalities (too bossy).

I thought I knew what I was doing when I retrained as a teacher as part of my mid-life crisis. Only after several years of teaching did I properly realise that I. Had. No. Idea.

I've never been someone who always knew what they wanted to be when they grew up. I'm a bit of an agnostic about free will anyway. I was very good at writing essays in exams and had excellent teachers. I went to a school that, despite a uniform that consisted of old-fashioned and unflattering tartan skirts and hats, expected students to rise above this handicap and do well. Obligingly, I obtained high marks at the end of Year 12. Somewhat ironically, my own teachers were horrified by the idea that I would consider teaching. My headmistress, who was the archetypical headmistress – tall with a ramrod posture, a firm bust and even firmer views, single, and completely devoted to her school – was also unimpressed by the idea.

Although our uniform was deliberately old-fashioned and

unflattering, insisting on dresses and on hats (I had only just missed out on having to wear the gloves), the school's attitude was otherwise progressive. We were expected to rise above the gendered expectations of our tartan skirts and achieve great things in the world.

It was an immense and expensive privilege to go to this school. The parent body was middle-class and professional, or people who wanted their child to be a middle-class professional, and who felt that private schooling was a route there. I am acutely aware of my good fortune in being able to attend this school, not least because of my father reminding me, as he did almost daily, that the decades-old Valiant he drove, our lack of new clothes and our lack of holidays anywhere except at our grandparents' house, was a direct result of the school fees he was paying. It was a choice he and my mother made, and in a better society, it would not even be an option or a decision they had to make or were even able to make. Plenty of great educational systems (I am of course looking at you, Finland) don't allow private schools. Plenty of excellent schools in Australia are public schools.

I am aware that I was a privileged white girl, blessed with the advantages that should, in a just society, be equally available to all, rather than those who wished to economically transmit privilege. I am also aware that this book is a collection of first-world problems and middle-class whining. It is a pity party for me, a woman who has everything and who is fortunate enough to be a member of the most privileged 1 per cent in the world. I know I can't check my privilege even by acknowledging it. All I can say in my defence is that this was, and this is, my setting and context. Context, as every English teacher will tell you, is everything. I'm also going to say one more thing (and then I'm going to try and stop addressing you directly, as if I have delusions that I am Charlotte Bronte): that people who never have any complaints and never whinge about anything might be saintly and good, but I don't really want to sit next to next to them at dinner. This, I must be clear, is a bitch-fest and I am wealthy, white and, well, a bitch, who is bitching about nothing at all really.

My headmistress held a personal exit interview with me (and, I must admit, with every other girl in my year). It was faintly alarming to be alone in the room with her, and even though I knew I did not have an illicit packet of cigarettes stashed in my locker, my palms were clammy and my heart pounded like a bass speaker in a nightclub.

She told me how lovely it was to see me (I'm still not sure if that was a dig, as I loathed co-curricular activities and team sports, and so was never up on stage at assembly to receive the merits she regularly handed out). She then asked what my plans were for next year.

'Well,' I squeaked, annoyingly nervous in her presence. 'I love English. It's my favourite subject. I was thinking of going to university to study Arts.'

'What a ridiculous waste,' said my headmistress, revealing that she did not to share Miss Jean Brodie's appreciation for English literature. I decided this was not a good time to discuss this critical observation. My adored English teacher would enjoy this moment when I relayed it later, I reflected, and tucked the thought away for later discussion.

My exam results, expectations and pride meant I ended up doing a double degree in Arts and Law. I graduated into the 1990s recession, with legal jobs and all professional jobs almost non-existent, and *Reality Bites* on video as a glamorous representation of the fate of my fellow educated Gen Xers, and our inability to get anything other than a McJob.

My summer clerking at a legal practice during the holidays (translation for those who did not study law in the 1990s is that this involved photocopying documents for a future trial in a hot stuffy room while earning no or minimal salary), had revealed the less than Ally McBeal reality of life as a worker bee in a law firm. A few years away from school had given me a fresh appreciation of teaching, and of the excellent teaching I had received at my school. Simultaneously scorned and rejected by the law, I saw teaching as my dream career to use my freshly minted and otherwise unusable Arts degree (joke of the era: 'What did the Arts/Law graduate say to the Med graduate?' Answer: 'Do you want fries with that?') I thought that by being an English teacher I could keep wallowing in the world of books, and I enrolled to do teaching as a post-graduate qualification.

Just as soon my enrolment in a graduate diploma of education had been accepted, and I had agreed to take on more student debt, fate spun the wheel on me again. I had spent the last year sending my CV to every law firm in the state, along with an individually tailored letter begging them to take me on as a junior solicitor. Just as I had resigned myself to the endless rejections, one of my applications finally resulted in a job interview and, as I failed to fuck it up in person, a graduate position at a law firm was offered to me. It was like hitting the jackpot, except statistically less likely.

I had previously scored several interviews which went appallingly for both me and the interview panel. For one interview, someone in a suit called me into his office in a shiny glass building and asked me to look at a towering pile of CVs, which I was assured, were all better than mine was. 'Look at the mound of applicants, each one from a brilliant young lawyer. I can't even leap over this pile. Why are you so special?' he asked, with what I desperately hoped was a rhetorical question. When I realised it wasn't, I assured my (much smaller) interlocutor that I could, in fact, actually leap over the pile. It wasn't the answer he was looking for. My black suit and I headed back down to ground level in the mirrored lift sooner than I had expected. I always found it hard to summon the correct level of enthusiasm for job interviews without sounding sarcastic. At another interview, for a property law job, I was asked how long I had wanted to do property law. My answer: 'Ever since I was a little girl, I have dreamed of practising property law,' sounded less than serious. Maybe the successful candidate had managed to elaborate on his childhood vision of bringing justice to the downtrodden by helping transact commercial property. Fortunately, I would never have to make chitchat with him in the office lunchroom and find out.

When I finally managed to sound properly serious, and presumably benefited from a series of extremely unfortunate events occurring to all the other suitable young lawyers in town, I was offered a job as a junior solicitor in a real firm. Legal jobs were the white whale for all graduates and so I declined my teaching training offer and headed into the law to become fully admitted as a solicitor and enjoy the prestigious glamour of wearing a black skirt suit and sheer black pantyhose every day, filling in timesheets, writing letters of advice, photocopying and working late every night. I then moved sideways into policy work, where there was less photocopying, no timesheets at all, and the happy ability to request legal advice from a solicitor and then request it again from another solicitor when you didn't like the advice you had initially received. Even better, you could ask for it all to be done by tomorrow and then go home for dinner while your solicitor did the late night for you.

It was only years later, after I had my children, that I was able to use my career break (and my surprise nine-month gap between pregnancies) to think about what it was I really wanted to do. I didn't want to head back to the office. At my last birthday, I had turned 37, a year older than my mother had been when she died. There's nothing like outliving a parent to make you do what you want to do right now, as you know there's no point in waiting for a tomorrow that might never come. I did really want to have the chance to be a teacher. I wanted to influence students' lives (for the better, I must clarify in this age of social influencers). I wanted to share my love of learning, my love of reading and writing. I wanted to make a difference and be that teacher who changed lives. It would be the most rewarding thing I could imagine to have even one student say that I'd taught them something, or inspired them to better things. At this stage, my influence on the world was writing memos that no-one read and that no-one would ever read. If I ever imagined my funeral, it would be hearing my husband say: 'She apparently wrote an okay memo, and she'd always planned to finish tidying the linen cupboard.'

I also figured I had the right sort of personality for teaching: I'm bossy, I like showing off my knowledge and I like helping people. I also very much like long holidays and enjoying a good work–life balance, and I dreamed of a job where I could spend more time with my children. I actually do like other people's children too. Once you can argue and reason with them. Secondary-school-aged children. Teaching seemed perfect.

So, thinking I knew exactly what I was signing up for, when my youngest child went to her early learning centre I decided to go back to university to do a quick Graduate Diploma of Education. It would take only a year; perfect for the person who hated commitment. I told myself that if I didn't enjoy my practice runs as a student teacher, then I would at least have scratched that itch, and could happily head back to the office, with an additional understanding of educational theory to add to my work in government policy. While at university, I would be in a world I was familiar with, even though I would now be the irritatingly keen mature-aged student instead of the irritatingly work-shy teenager. I thought that my time at school as a student meant that I knew what being a teacher would entail. In this, like so much else in life, I was wrong.

Learning to be a teacher by attending lectures is a bit like learning to cook by watching someone stand in front of you and tell you what cooking is like. It's dry and theoretical. You really need to see the teaching happening and see how the students react to that teaching. Teaching, as a wise teacher once said to me, is really a trade, and he was right. You learn by feeling the heat in the kitchen and by getting burnt occasionally. The most important part of our teacher training was the teaching placements. They were crucial to becoming a teacher. One student in our year returned from her first placement with the valuable insight that she didn't really like teenagers. When we pressed her for more details, fascinated, a little bit horrified and awfully impressed with her honesty, she said she liked the concept of teenagers, but the reality of being stuck in a room with them all day was quite a different thing. 'And,' she continued, 'have we ever noticed the overpowering smell of feet?'

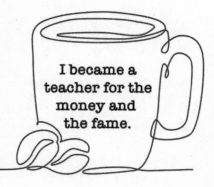

I became a
teacher for the
money and
the fame.

3

FAKE IT UNTIL YOU MAKE IT

I was excited about how much better university would be the second time around, in the twenty-first century. Due to my maternal commitments, I only appeared on campus during O week (this is short for Orientation week but 'O week' sounds cheeringly less like compasses will be needed) to purchase the prescribed textbooks from the university book shop. I loyally did this even though I, and every graduate, knows that textbooks are only set on book lists so lecturers can increase sales of their own backlist. There's something about the wild enthusiasm of shopping a booklist that will never be matched by the actual desire to read the books. In the university bookshop I mooched about, seduced by displays of unchewed pens and Moleskine notebooks. When I left the store, burdened with my shopping, I looked about excitedly. They say you can't go back. I found out the hard way that you can, but you'll be fat, old and wearing the wrong clothes. The musty scent of nostalgia is one of those smells that gives you a slight headache, which might explain why I found everything and everyone so wanting.

When I was an undergraduate, O week was a riot of bands, subsidised beer and ill-thought-out choices. It was fun and frivolous. You could visit all the clubs and activity stalls and there were older, sophisticated students handing out showbags with brochures, chocolates, condoms and the first dental dam I'd ever seen. It's still the only dental dam I've ever seen. My university life failed to live up to the hedonistic heights promised by O week. There were pub crawls, there were drinks and there were many regrets. I made the sort of friends who would happily talk with me all the way through a property law lecture. When I had duly graduated as a lawyer and was proudly sitting alone in my glass cubicle office at my big desk, in a glass tower in what passes for the city centre in Adelaide, my desk phone rang. (That's how long ago it was. I did not have a mobile phone.) It was a friend from university with whom I had happily talked throughout all our lectures. We started comparing notes about the practical challenges of our new jobs. A highlight was our mutual moaning about our inability to instantly recall, in client meetings or phone calls, the finer details of the law. My friend amusingly and accurately complained: 'If I'd known it was going to be so important I'd have paid attention at the time. But it was so dull it seemed that there was no way it could be important.' Needless to say, that friend is now a highly esteemed and expert lawyer with a firm grasp of all of the details after his time in practice.

Modern O week had a bland corporate air that jelled with the bland corporate students, sadly already aspiring to a responsible life. To be fair, they were crippled with debt, under whatever acronym the Australian Government was currently using to justify charging citizens for things that a first-world nation should provide for free, such as further education. We were not in a learning environment of dreaming spires and students finding themselves. Instead, we were in the drab world of consumers, loans and economic rationalism. There were tidy queues of neatly dressed, well-groomed students holding lots of expensive IT. They were clutching takeaway cups of coffee and bottles of water. One even had a rolled-up umbrella. Some boys had briefcases. There were still O week showbags being handed out. After explaining that I wasn't someone's mum, but a real student myself, I was grudgingly handed a bag. It tuned out that it wasn't worth the humiliation, as it contained reams of brochures and a small lunchbox-sized bag of Barbeque Shapes. After looking through the bag I joked, 'Not even a free set of steak knives?' The student looked at me blankly and I belatedly realised that this was a joke from a time when people watched advertisements on the TV. It was from a time when people watched TV. It was from a time when people made bad jokes, rather than memes. I handed the bag back to the student. 'You can recycle this one,' I said, and he beamed.

At uni, I was clearly too old and crusty to sit with the recent undergraduates. They were perky, enthusiastic and mostly didn't drink. In a tutorial group one day a girl confided that it was her twenty-first birthday. Excitedly, I offered to take her to the university tavern for a drink to celebrate this milestone over our lunch break. She confessed that she didn't know where the tavern was. It's always unbearable to tell people that they have wasted their time at university, but of course I had to do so.

There was another cluster of students who were all around their late twenties or early thirties. These were nearly all artsy, theatrical or musical types, who had spent their twenties giving it a red-hot go, and who were now getting a teaching qualification as a back-up. They were kind, fun and not at all interested in spending time with old farts like me. They tended towards dramatic hair and displayed a healthy balance between cynicism and enthusiasm. The art, music and drama departments of Australian schools would be lucky to have them. Then there were the mummies and oldies like me. Some of us were career changers fleeing from the office, some retirees, and others were going to go absolutely berserk if they spent any more time working silently in a lab. The common thread was that everyone was a good egg. They were responsible types. No-one was going to steal your student ID card and use it to send a scan of their bare arse around the uni. They made me feel, vaguely and guiltily, like I was not good enough to be one of them.

The innate goodness of teachers was something that continually surprised me. When I attended my first professional conference for English teachers, where speakers were offered their choice of a thank-you gift of either a half case of wine for themselves or a clutch of textbooks for their school, every single teacher chose some books for their school. I was open-mouthed with surprise. If you'd offered something similar to lawyers, they'd have pulled out the first cork before they had returned to their seat. Teachers are so good, so happy to help, that it is no wonder they are trampled all over, paid so little and so poorly regarded by society. It's probably also why the profession, being a caring profession, is so female dominated. Women are socialised to put themselves last, and so teaching is a natural expansion of that.

Our university lecture halls were crowded, and we were treated to hour-long lectures, many of them un-ironically devoted to explaining how hard it is to concentrate during and retain information from a lengthy lecture. Rather than providing compelling lectures, our attendance was compelled by a sign-in sheet. The good teachers all dutifully signed in, meaning that the rest of us also had to do so. I'm confident (although the rosy haze of nostalgia might be tinting this prediction) that if you tried to pull that stunt at my left-wing undergraduate university campus the sign-in sheet would have been completed by twenty Ms NoneOfYourBusiness and ten Mr Donald Ducks.

Teaching courses are crowded. Teaching students are cheap to have on campus as they don't need laboratories or any special resources so the universities can pile them high. Even better, the actual practicalities of teaching are taught by other unpaid proper schoolteachers while the teaching students are on placement at a real school. Teaching is also an easy course for students to apply for, with minimal pre-requisites and no aptitude testing involved. Teaching courses also accept students with low ATAR scores, to the annual horror of the media. The same media that denigrates teachers at every opportunity is of course the same one that likes to attack the ATAR scores of applicants for teaching. Usually with a headline like 'Failures teach our kids'. As a student in the education faculty you are part of the huddled masses on campus, the 'boring majority'. It's a good preparation for your future profession as a teacher where you will pull your own socks up and make the best of what you get.

My teaching lecturers were the usual mix of academics that I had already encountered as an undergraduate student (observed of course by me, a typical 'type' of student too, the smartarse cynic who not-so-secretly thinks she is above all of this). They included:

• The true academic researching some esoteric topic that has no application except for improving the university's research ratings. Easily identified by their unhelpful lectures filled with impenetrable jargon. They were serious ivory tower inhabitants, untroubled by the realities of school life.

• The ex-teaching practitioners who had retreated to the sheltered workshop of tertiary education. My favourite was the one who spent a semester on work that was no longer part of the Australian curriculum and who made us submit three pointless assignments. Eventually our tutorial group set up a private Facebook group to try to decipher what work he actually wanted from us. At least having him at university meant that he was no longer teaching defenceless school students.

• The jaded cynic (needless to say I loved him). He told us teaching could not make a difference, and we'd be spending our lives battling poor parenting and society that didn't value young people.

- The inspired practitioner. I should have loved her, as she spent her time telling us how life-changing a good teacher could be and talked about the power of education to shape lives. She had moved into academia to inspire broader change.

- The pragmatist. Dabbling in academia and still teaching. Busy, overworked but providing useful and practical advice. Our lessons on behaviour management and the psychology of learning were fascinating and should have been given much more time in the syllabus.

I had finally got into the rhythm of university life when the first school placement came up. It was apparent from the way the lecturers spoke at university that we would learn everything about teaching from actually teaching. It seemed reasonable as I had not learned that much from my coursework.

Each student had to complete two placements, each five weeks long, and receive a passing grade and survive an inspection from the university in order to finish the course. We were told that we needed to undertake one placement in a country school and one in a city school. Students who knew the system (as children of teachers, or with teaching friends) had already begun scheming to arrange placements at schools that were technically 'country' but were really on the fringes of suburbia.

My teaching friends had been scattered widely throughout the state for their placements. The one mantra passed around like gospel by all the students and that was reiterated by all the lecturers (a consensus like this was an extremely rare occurrence), was the need do an amazing and impressive job on the school campus. The most reliable way to get that elusive first teaching contract was to get an offer from a school where you did your placement. In fact, rumour had it, this was the only way to get a teaching contract. We were told to be cheerful, reliable, unflappable and to volunteer for absolutely every task. So, no pressure then.

I spent the weekend before my first placement stress-buying some new teacher-appropriate clothes. My old black suits (which didn't fit me anymore, anyway) were generally agreed to be too formal and off-putting, especially for someone who was older than their supervising teacher. We were advised to look neat and tidy and to dress modestly, with no denim and no flesh on view. Understandably, we also spent the week before our first placement being talked through the legal and ethical minefields of teaching. This made for an unusually interesting and relevant set of lectures. A lawyer who specialised in the area was even drafted in to speak to us, and so was a teacher's union representative. The focus was on avoiding inappropriate relationships with students. We were told not to befriend students on social media until they had left school, not to socialise with students, not to sit alone with them in a classroom with a closed door, and not to touch them whatever happened. For once, the tutorials were vibrant as we all swapped gossipy stories about inappropriate teachers we had known and the salacious details of the recent legal cases.

I felt sorry for the younger students, the ones who were just twenty or twenty-one. They were still roughly in the peer group age of Year 12 students, and it would be harder for them to avoid interacting with students. For once, being an old fat hag felt like a massive societal advantage. Being in my thirties meant that all school students would see me as an ancient crone. It was unlikely anyone would want to befriend me or flirt with me.

4

SCHOOL DAZE

The night before my first teaching placement turned out to be like every other night in my life before school started. As I wasn't yet an English teacher, I hadn't instinctively identified this as foreshadowing, but it was an ominous portent of how teaching would make me, in many ways, a slave to school rhythm again. I couldn't go to sleep, and then woke repeatedly to nervously check that my alarm clock was properly switched on. I am a resolutely not a lark and I always have a second wind (for tidying, completing work, reading two more chapters of my book, binge-watching crap on television or reading the internet on my phone) at around 10pm. This is also the body clock of almost all teenagers and so it seems ridiculous that school starts so early in the morning. I was expected to be in the classroom at 8.15am and had been advised to get to school by 8am by the very latest. My children's heroic out-of-school hours childcare opened at 7am so I was, in theory at least, able to drop them off early to get to the school on time.

The morning of my first placement I put on my modest teaching clothes (skirt below the knee, no cleavage), comfortable shoes (this is not a challenge, as I have been blessed with six feet of height, so all my shoes are comfortable shoes) and loaded up my bag with a laptop and my stationery. I had proudly saved all the lesson plans I had prepared at university onto my laptop and was confident that I had lots of resources up my sleeve. I dropped the children off and then drove on to my school to find a park. Parking is always a problem for city and suburban schools, and I had been instructed not to park in the teacher's car park (oversubscribed already), not to park in the streets near the school (filled with complaining people who had unaccountably bought property next to a school and hated every effect the school had on their street except for the increase in house prices) and to instead find a safe and distant park and hike in to work. I say work, but of course as a student teacher I wasn't being paid. This was fair enough, as I knew nothing and bought nothing to the school. I should have been paying them.

I wandered in through the school grounds at the moment that it always looks most perfect —when there are no students and the maintenance men (they are always men, just like the way the uniform shop is always filled with women) had cleaned up yesterday's mess. Struggling to orient myself, despite the orange school logo and crest shouting from a cacophony of surfaces, I found the front office, signed myself in with the lovely school receptionist and went to find the Vice Principal.

At that time, one of the many, many things I did not know

about private schools was that the Vice Principal (or Deputy Head) is always the workhorse of the school, the member of management who gets everything done. The Principal (or Headmaster/Headmistress) is the show pony, with good hair. They are well paid and therefore have lovely clothes and good cars (a rarity for a teacher). Their presentation and persuasive skills are all-important as they have to sweet-talk the families of prospective students, lead fundraising drives, write and deliver speeches at assemblies, create content for newsletters and make the high-level decisions at innumerable late-night meetings. The Vice Principal is the one who deals with the students who are found with vodka and e-cigarettes at camp, the students who are self-harming, have eating disorders, are sick, are moving house, whose parents are fighting it out in the courts, the students who are rude and disruptive in class and those who cannot be persuaded to do any schoolwork. Then there are the issues of teachers who quit, get pregnant or break their arms on camp, as well as battling all the latest educational initiatives and funding hoops imposed by the tangle of bodies who control schools. The Vice Principal is also the person who deals with the plague of student teachers that descend on campus twice a year, creating endless paperwork and administrative headaches. Vice Principals never want to have a student teacher on campus but are usually too diplomatic to say so. Teaching is also a career of sacrifice for the greater good and taking on a student teacher who will be nothing but a burden for the whole of their placement is part of this sacrifice, and testament to the essential saintly nature at the heart of all Vice Principals.

This Vice Principal was in the mould of every other Vice Principal I would meet. Kind, practical, distracted by her huge workload, and toiling away in a small unglamorous office almost overflowing with piles of paper that all needed her urgent attention. The office was in the heart of the action (the Principal's office is deliberately more inaccessible; the Vice Principal is placed somewhere close where they can be bothered for every crisis). She had an endearingly messy ponytail and managed to brief me while a woman (who I later learned was the relief-teacher manager) kept popping into the office with tales of flu, conjunctivitis, bad backs, sick children and bus companies who didn't know where they were meant to be twenty minutes ago.

'So, you want to be a teacher?' she said, sounding mildly confused as she obviously re-read my CV on her computer email. 'Are you sure? There looks like there is lots else you can do?'

Primed by the need to impress her and to secure a job offer, I launched into my prepared speech about wanting to inspire a love of learning and a devotion to literature, and to change the lives of young people forever.

'That's lovely,' she said. 'How nice.' And she gave me a sweet smile, the one I imagine she used when she saw pictures of kittens sleeping or her pigeonhole empty of papers. The smile then retreated, to be replaced by a worried look.

'Now, I'm low on staff for yard duty all week and was wondering if you wouldn't mind doing the first half of lunch every day. I'm sure we can sort something out next week.'

'Yes, of course' I said, keen to prove that I could accept responsibility. 'Anything I can do to help.'

'Lovely,' she said, rapidly clicking through documents on screen. 'Your university wants you to observe for the first week and then teach a lesson in one of your three subjects every day for the next four weeks. That will give you a half-time load. In the last week, I have to organise a time when the university will send someone out to watch you teach a lesson. Don't worry, it will be fine.

'First of all ... are you Ms or Mrs?'

'A Mrs,' I said.

'Mrs Brooks,' she said out loud. I was startled, like the first time I heard my new married name called out by the pharmacist. Then, I had stupidly looked around, wondering at the coincidence that had my mother-in-law in my local pharmacy picking up a script at the same time as me. Teachers, who have so little else, have clung on the honorific of Mr or Mrs, and are the only people in our society still addressed this way. It does have its benefits, as when someone greets me as 'Mrs Brooks' I know that I must have taught them, which sadly only narrows them down to about a thousand likely candidates and does not really improve the odds that I will remember their name. I am a bad person.

'Your subjects are English, History and Legal studies? Is that right?'

'Yes,' I agreed. I wanted to launch into my imposter syndrome speech about how I didn't feel worthy to teach these subjects, but managed to bite this back.

'We have excellent teachers in all those areas. You will need to spend time with as many year levels as possible. Let's print off a timetable for you.'

She printed off a blank timetable from her overworked printer and then, looking at her screen and at reams of data, swiftly assembled a timetable for me, scribbling in every space the name of a teacher and a classroom code. She wrote in my yard duty and then handed the timetable over to me. I had forgotten how many lessons school students had in a day. There was also assembly and roll call. When I'd thought about being a teacher, I hadn't considered these as an aspect of my workday.

She told me the names of the three teachers who would supervise my three subjects and said that she would take me along to the staffroom to introduce me to them. She accompanied me out of her office, proudly pointing out a collage on the wall prepared as a gift by the last year's graduating class, before she was interrupted by various members of the school administration team requesting her urgent opinion on a number of bubbling disasters. I then got a brief pep talk about the history of the school and the dress and behavioural expectations for teachers before she apologetically sent me into the hall while she went back to her office and took a phone call from an aggrieved mother who was outraged that her daughter had only got a B for her last assignment and wanted the teacher responsible for this catastrophe to be sacked.

I sat in the hall on a wooden bench, the sort that I recognised from my old school days as the one for naughty students to sit on while they waited for a mighty telling off from the Vice Principal. I immediately felt young and vaguely guilty, and started wondering what I had done wrong. Even though it wasn't my old school, I felt almost as if I had been here before, and experienced an almost Proustian moment, not quite déjà vu, from the squeaky lino on the floor, the black scuff marks on the walls, the flickering fluorescent lights, the relentlessly colourful posters advertising upcoming school events, and the crisp lemon with a hint of vomit smell, coming from what I imagined was the detergent used to mop the floors. When the Vice Principal came out to join me, I felt about thirteen years old again. I even could feel an anxiety-induced pimple sprouting on my chin, just to complete the whole vibe.

'Sorry about that,' she apologised. 'Gap between expectations and reality. Child is not setting the world on fire, but she and the mother think otherwise. I am sure she deserved less than a B. It will be hell when she gets to the end of Year 12.'

I felt shocked. Where was the jargon I had been so recently taught, the coy euphemisms to use like 'intellectual underachiever'?

'Dad's reasonable, and I think he sees the situation for what it is but his wife has fantasies that her daughter is a future Nobel prize winner. Let's go, and I'll give a quick tour on the way.'

I started to worry if I would ever be able to find my way to any of the classrooms, as she led me down maze-like hallways and strange staircases, past endless rooms that all looked the same and only a small orange number painted on the doors to distinguish them. It was disorienting and strange, like being toured through my son's Minecraft worlds, and just as cubic and unreal. We walked through the library, past the toilet blocks and finally arrived at the staffroom, tucked away in a corner of a huge building. As we had walked along, I was impressed that she greeted every student we passed by name, saying good morning and stopping for a longer chat with about ten individual students to talk about recent achievements such as a music exam, an excellent debate or winning goal in Saturday's match. It was awe-inspiring and made me realise firstly that the Vice Principal must be out every night of the week watching her students do their special things, and secondly, that with my woeful inability to recall names, I was probably never going to be a good teacher.

We continued down the hall, with the Vice Principal instinctively picking up pieces of rubbish from the floor, and straightening notices on the pin-up boards without breaking her stride. Finally, we reached an unobtrusive blue door marked 'Staffroom'. At just past 8am the room was buzzing with teachers. They were making coffee, checking their pigeonholes, chatting and laughing. The smell of camaraderie, fresh perfume and Nescafé Blend 43 were in the air. I was wheeled around and introduced to them all while I panicked mildly that now I had even more names I would fail to remember at recess.

After experiencing a few more staffrooms, and more teacher observations during my student placements, I would eventually be able to manage to match teachers to their subject by their physical appearance (even if I was still crap at names). I am a bit ashamed of this blatant stereotyping by subject, but not as much as I should be. Now, after several years working in schools and hanging out in staffrooms, here is my handy cut-and-keep guide to help identify different teachers:

• Colourful clothes, large plastic jewellery, gorgeously applied makeup, esoteric conversation – art teachers.

• Long hair (all genders), anxious expression, flowing

outfits you've never seen in a shop, great gossip and knowledge of current films, TV, theatre productions and pop culture – drama teachers.

• Sing-song voices, patient, kind, absurdly youthful looking and with good hair – primary school teachers.

• Beards and/or ethnic jewellery, intense conversation about current issues covered recently by the ABC or *The Guardian* – geography teachers.

• Looks and dresses like an air hostess – French language teachers.

• Cardigans, short-sleeved shirts, mostly silent – maths teachers (except for the occasional tall, svelte, glamorous character who can't be otherwise placed and usually teaches a second, non-mathematical subject).

• Shorts (whatever the weather), sneakers, smoking hot body depressingly counteracted by a whistle on a chain worn around the neck like an accessory, foghorn voice, laughing, joking and making coffee for hours – PE teachers.

• Sensible shoes, intense stare, ability to explain lesson allocations according to Union requirements and school employment agreements, polite, kind and not usually swept up in the staffroom politics – science teachers.

• Anxious face, stooped back and shoulders, lovely jewellery and too busy to chat, but with some quite good conversation when pressed – English teachers.

• Causes everyone to leave the room when they arrive – member of teaching management who assigns relief lessons.

• Well groomed, never seen in prints or patterns,

impeccably made-up, never runs – Principal, Head of Senior School or Junior School.

• Invisible – history teachers due to current overwhelming desire to study subjects that are more business focused. No-one is (I think) yet teaching a subject called 'become a middle-management cubicle dweller' but it must be coming soon.

In my first staffroom (and in fact in every subsequent staffroom) everyone was kind, interested in me and offered to help out. Faced with such generosity and sweetness, I almost cried. A few even questioned me, with a knowing smile, about the latest trends in teacher training, and yelped in recognition when I described what the university had told me about teaching.

'It's all useless,' they explained, kindly. 'Just pay attention here and you will be fine.'

One particularly lovely woman (obviously self-sacrificing as she had clearly agreed to be burdened with me, something that no overworked teacher would ever want to do) was introduced as the English teacher who would be my lead supervisor and the Vice Principal left me in her care. She was called Mrs X and, I later discovered, was a seasoned soldier who knew where all the bodies were buried. She pointed out the staff loos and firmly advised me to 'go now' as female teacher toilets and toilet breaks were thin on the ground.

Teachers continued to pile into the room until 8.15am when a loud bell started ringing, causing me to flinch and spill my coffee. Mrs X laughed. 'You'll get used to that,' she said. 'We think it's to wake up the Seniors. Let's go,' and she gathered up piles of papers and headed out to her form room.

At most Australian schools, only primary school teachers generally have the luxury of staying in the same classroom for most of the day. Everyone else has to troop from room to room, clutching their essentials like a harried international traveller, subject to the vagaries of the timetable.

As a side note, it took me years as a teacher to appreciate the skill of the generally unsung member of teaching management who writes the timetable. As often in life, it wasn't until a bumbler was unfortunately left with control of the timetable one semester and subjects had to be dropped from the schedule, teachers lost their free lessons and practical science lessons were put in normal classrooms, that I truly appreciated the ramifications of proper timetabling for efficiently running a school.

Arranging the timetable is a dark art, requiring one mere mortal to combine the skills of an air traffic controller, a mathematician, a logistics expert and a psychologist. It is usually performed by a non-descript teacher in a back office, who emerges blinking into the light twice a year, clutching a new timetable for the semester that has taken weeks of time and litres of sweat to achieve. The new timetable is never praised, only complained about by staff and students. Creating a timetable to suit everyone is an almost impossible aim, like shopping for your brother-in-law for Christmas. There are always too few classrooms, too many students, too many subjects and an abundance of public holiday Mondays that will wreck the delivery of each Year 12 course if given half a chance.

Timetabling also needs to account for the unquantified, but deeply powerful, rhythms of the school week. In schools, much as is the case for many workplaces, Friday is the least productive day of the week. The sunny Monday that starts off every week is burnished with good intentions from staff and students. Monday morning is the most scholastically focused section of the week and the first two lessons are generally the most academically worthwhile. Scholarly enthusiasm gradually slides during the week and Fridays are decidedly patchy. In the same way, the ability of students to learn and concentrate is governed by a hidden yet powerful tide – which is highest in the morning and gradually ebbs away during the day. A lesson after lunch can achieve only half as much as a lesson before recess. Working parents who endlessly wail 'why can't school go on until 5pm or even 5.30pm' not only have school confused with childcare, but also have never seen how their own little darlings behave in a classroom after 2pm, when they are slumped, unresponsive and glassy-eyed on a desk, capable of breathing and nothing else. Those of you who have seen the scene in the movie *Ferris Bueller's Day Off* where the student sleeps drooling on the desk have a mental picture ready to use here. 'Danke Schoen' (just in case you need a soundtrack for that picture too).

The ideal timetable would be able to respond to these rhythms, along with the other competing timetabling demands. The mornings would be filled with the harder subjects (everyone knows what these are, even though schools and curriculum bodies like to pretend that all subjects are equal) and the school day would get less rigorous as it went on. Friday afternoons, the nadir of school time, would be devoted to unchallenging subjects like PE, Personal Development or, at religion-based schools, whatever is the latest culturally inclusive phrase for religious education.

The perfect timetable would also ensure that assemblies (notorious for going over time, as teachers, who are used to holding forth for an hour at a time, find it hard to deliver pithy updates about the latest Charity Day once they have control of the microphone) would all be held before lunch, or before a worthless and infinitely elastic Friday afternoon subject.

Timetabling also requires attention to Mondays, as the Monday public holidays that occur frequently during the first semester of Australian schools can strip a poorly timetabled school of a valuable chunk of lesson time, particularly if the harder Year 12 subjects have double lessons on Mondays. Some school timetablers have adopted the two-week timetable, with a rotation between Week A and Week B to deal with these interruptions to the school week. The seven-day week and five-day work week must have an innate connection to human brain as no-one can ever remember a ten-day timetable. This means that schools with a Week A (for the first alternate week) and Week B (for the second) erupt into a bleating mess at the change of every lesson, as everyone asks plaintively to the rest of the flock 'what lesson do we have now?' and no student ever manages to remember to bring in their gear for PE.

The poor timetablers also have to give teachers a free lesson every day, purely to allow them to go to the loo at least once, as recess and lunch time can involve yard duty, meetings, emails, marking, lesson prep and meeting with students to help with their work. (Plus the daily spare lesson is the one the school uses to nab teachers to cover their colleagues who are away sick or on camp or an excursion.) Finally, the timetable also must account for part-time teachers, as well as balancing the workloads of other full-time teachers. Most schools try and limit the number of Year 12 classes that can be taken by one teacher, as Year 12 is the year with the neediest students and parents.

I rushed along beside Mrs X, who cheerfully chided passing students about late work as we went to her form room. I kept looking at my new timetable, trying to work out where I needed to be all day. We swung into Mrs X's classroom, which I couldn't helping noting looked exactly like my classroom when I was at school over twenty years ago, except for an electronic whiteboard instead of a blackboard. There was the same sort of ugly uncomfortable brown plastic chairs, dusty windows that offered views to nowhere and scuffed dark carpet that looked as though it had lived a hard life; the floor covering equivalent of Keith Richards.

Groups of well-groomed students sat on the edges of their desks, chatting happily. To a girl, they all had long, glossy ponytails (which any show pony would covet), stylishly shaped eyebrows, flawless complexions, tanned legs, foundation, blusher, mascara and blended eye shadow in discreet defiance of the school's 'no makeup' policy. I had been congratulating myself on applying my tinted SPF moisturiser before I left the house that morning, as well as applying another squirt of dry shampoo to my hair that was now more dry shampoo than hair. I had also applied lipstick from a semi-melted tube in the glovebox of my car just after I had found a park. But now I instantly felt ungroomed, ungainly and ancient. And, I must admit, a little sad that this selfie-taking generation had to look good at all times, as it must mean they could never relax, always anxious that their image might be shared worldwide. I am eternally grateful that there are only about three photos of me that record my time as a teenager. The boys were more reassuringly normal; they looked younger, pimplier and more like the children they were.

The students cheerfully greeted Mrs X, and she introduced me to the class. They turned their laser focus on to me and blatantly looked me up and down, clearly finding me a disappointment. I curled my fingers to try and mask my bitten nails. Mrs X went to her desk, the students sat at their desks and instantly the first awkwardness of being an observer was apparent – where to sit? Up the front where everyone would stare at me, or at the back where I would be awkwardly closer and probably too close to the students? Mrs X was plugging on with the morning, so I pulled an empty chair away from its desk and sat in the aisle, hoping to be ignored by the class.

Mrs X took the roll, engaged in some banter with a latecomer (who glared at me, making me feel guilty about taking what was obviously his usual seat) and then ran through an incredibly long list of notices for the day: choirs, sports, debating, lost clothes, fund raising and clubs. The list was so long that Mrs X was still talking her way through it when the bell rang. A bell ringing suggests a tuneful peal from the bell tower or the smooth chirrup of an old-fashioned phone. This school bell didn't really ring so much as it clanged, with a sound that put my teeth on edge and felt like the start of a headache. Clearly, however, like the Hunchback of Notre Dame, who I felt was my soulmate, I would have to get used to loud bells. The students ambled out to their first lesson and I anxiously looked at my timetable. I was hugely relieved that I was to stay with the comforting Mrs X.

She gathered up her stuff again and led me along the maze of corridors to another classroom. Again, all was familiar except for the electronic whiteboard, and this time I noticed a projector bolted to the roof. I made some inane comment about the whiteboard and Mrs X told me not to worry, that everyone just used them like a normal whiteboard. They had been a wildly fashionable must-have, all teachers had endured compulsory training about them, to explain the 'functionality' no teacher had ever asked for, and then everyone stopped bothering with the technology and just used them as a bog-standard whiteboard.

Mrs X told me the novel the class was studying, which I had never read before. She handed me her copy and settled me in at my own desk at the back of the classroom. The students filed in and, after a quick glance in my direction, ignored me. The lesson started and I admired Mrs X's neat, round handwriting as she wrote on the whiteboard. It made me instantly think of my own untidy scrawl. A (male) law partner who I worked for aeons ago had once scathingly remarked that I 'had the untidiest handwriting he had ever seen for a woman', providing further assurance, not that any more was needed, that female solicitors were held to a different standard than male solicitors. I have truly illegible handwriting and had never properly considered that calligraphy was a requirement for teachers. In fact, as Mrs X ran through the apparently terrible essay plans her students had submitted, I realised that not once while studying teaching had we been instructed or required to demonstrate our skills in writing on a whiteboard or even engaging a classroom of students. There had been a lot on the what to do, but not so much on the how to do it.

I looked around the class and noted that the students were, unsurprisingly, sitting in their friendship groups. Student cliques are a fact of life, and teachers need to decide what, if anything, they will do about them. Many teaching textbooks and Facebook posts (teaching strategy is all shared by social media) talk about cliques as though they are as terrifying as a Covid outbreak. In fact, a clique is an unshakable aspect of human life. In every group of people, you will try to hang out with those you like. Even at a family funeral you will naturally gravitate to the fun cousins rather than the boring ones. Cliques during teenage years can, however, be particularly cruel. There is nothing on earth as bitchy as a group of fourteen-year-old girls who want to be popular. In the jostling for the role of Queen Bee, they will destroy anyone. One option for teachers who want to try to minimise the pain of cliques is the introduction of a seating plan. Or not. There are pros and cons for each.

A classroom with no seating plan
A lack of a plan disregards all attempts to arrange and let students sit where they want to. This treats students like adults (or at least almost like sentient beings) and often results in a happy classroom. Students get to sit with people they like, and not with any possible tormentors. Plus, it is one less thing for a teacher to try to organise,

and they have enough on their plates without making sure that so-and-so is in their designated seat. If I did go with this relaxed approach (and I tend to as I was too lazy to enforce a seating plan, which takes at least two weeks of solid effort and rigorous enforcement), I always made sure that I selected the students for any pair or group work. Otherwise, someone would always be left out and, as a non-sporty person who no-one ever wanted on their team, I completely feel the pain of exclusion. Also, if the teacher doesn't organise the pairs or groups there will inevitably be one group where all the members are less academically gifted (insert current euphemism here) and they will struggle to cope with the more challenging tasks and potentially will be humiliated. Life is hard enough without being made to feel bad at school. Instead, those kids need to be scattered through the class groups, like sultanas in a hot cross bun.

A classroom with a seating plan

As mentioned above, a seating plan can take about two weeks of solid effort to enforce. Some teachers spend hours at home organising the seating plan for each class, sweating over it like it is the table plan for their wedding. They try to put the troublemakers up close and split up talkative and easily distractable friends, and then disaster invariably occurs mid-term when an episode of bullying or bitching erupts and two newly sworn enemies are required to sit next to each other.

Using an alphabetical seating plan is a safer logical

option, and I have noticed that maths teachers often use this. It makes taking the roll easy, and also helps the teacher quickly learn the names of the students. The special needs units of schools encourage teachers to sit students living with hearing or vision issues at the front of the class. However, in practice, most of these students are sick of being singled out and want to lurk anonymously in the middle row of the classroom.

If there is no seating allocation, it can be a revealing anthropological study to identify and categorise students based on where they chose to sit in the classroom.

The back row is invariably filled with the naughty, the troublemakers and the talkative. They thrive in a classroom that is so tightly packed that the teacher cannot walk around the room and stand behind them to see what they are really up to. The back row of the classroom is the less mobile equivalent of the back row of a school bus. It's where the rowdiness and the noise starts but it can also be the source of the fun in the classroom. If you can get the back row engaged in your lesson, then you are doing something right. Occasionally a pair of bright and naughty students decide to hide in plain sight and will deliberately chose to sit front and centre, wisely figuring that the teacher will be focused on the back row and will overlook them. Otherwise, the front row is selected by the diligent and interested students, the ones who are a joy to teach.

The only challenging student in the front row is the one who thinks they need to ask for help about everything, loudly and persistently, every three minutes. They've sat up the front so that they can monopolise your time more effectively. They are like the boring man from accounts at the office Christmas party who bails you up for hours while you keep trying to move away to the fun communications team without hurting his feelings. These students need everything explained at least twenty times, not for assistance, but for comfort. They will repeatedly stop you mid-sentence when you are teaching to ask something like: 'Miss, can you please just read over my first sentence? I can't do anything else without your help.' These students often like you, and will tell you so repeatedly, but human nature is a strange thing and, much like an overly keen date, you will often find it hard to reciprocate their enthusiasm. This student is, however, ideal for helping with any school admin that crops up during the lesson, as they are absolutely trustworthy and will never use time out of the classroom to spend five minutes on their phones scrolling TikTok. Plus, having them out of the room gives you and the other students a little break. When someone needs to go and fetch IT, get a maintenance man to remove a Huntsman spider, or escort a student who feels faint to the sick bay, the keen bean from the front row is the ideal candidate. And, rather sweetly, they are always happy to help.

The middle of the classroom is where the middle-of-the-range students sit, the nondescript ones who cause you no anguish but unfairly you occasionally have trouble remembering exactly who they are at Parent–Teacher

Interview nights. They are the forgotten and overlooked middle. Some groovy classrooms have a central round table, or mini horseshoe, lending the classroom a 'Knights of the Round Table' air; some have grouped tables, making the classroom look like a bad wedding venue but, despite the quirks, you can always find a 'front', 'back row' and 'middle' section even if those kids are more there in spirit than in placement.

There are also some empty seats in every classroom. Each class will have one student who absolutely loves the sick bay and is always either at the sick bay or asking you if they can go to the sick bay because they feel dizzy or headachy or another non-specific ailment. They have frequent flyer status with the school nurses and often have their 'own' favourite beds in the sick bay. The other empty seat in the class is the student who 'has gone to the toilet, Miss.' This is a trick I used at school myself, where I loathed French. I learned one sentence, *'Excusez-moi Mademoiselle, est-ce je peux allez au toilettes?'* When I received the answering *'Oui'* (wee jokes were the only fun to be had in French), I would head out to our locker room and spend the lesson peacefully reading a novel. In English, obviously.

I spent my first lesson as an observer in a classroom, huddled as near to the back row section as I could, wrestling with my face, trying to compose it into the correct expression. It is hard to be an adult in a roomful of children and look interested, but not inappropriately interested.

Mrs X, I was interested to note, had an ESP kind of

awareness of trouble in back row, and the ability to sense off-task behaviour before it really got off task. Her teacher radar was astounding and she had the ability (often displayed by mothers as well) to be taking part in one conversation while intently eavesdropping on two other conversations happening in the background. She finally finished distributing the essay plans, gave the class a motivational pep talk and set them off to work on their essays. Just as the lesson was getting into the swing of things, the bell rang. I flinched, and the students calmly started packing up to go to their next class.

Mrs X directed me to my next classroom, where I sat, observing, again hopefully not too creepily, a history lesson from the back row. Once more, it was masterclass in all the small details that I hadn't appreciated were so important. Both teachers made it look easy, fun even, and they never referred to a note or pre-prepared sheet. They had mastery of their content and their delivery. The history teacher then kindly took me back to the staffroom for recess, where I realised that I should have bought my own mug in from home. I tried to find the most anonymous mug to use from a sea of garish 'World's Best Teacher' and 'Congratulations' mugs. One teacher saw me anxiously sorting through the cupboard.

'They are all the end-of-year teacher presents,' she explained. 'In primary schools, often the whole class club together and get the teacher an expensive gift voucher. In senior schools, where we spend hours each week slaving over their marking, occasionally you get a mug or chocolates at the end of the year.'

'That's nice,' I said, as I looked at the dispiriting containers of no-brand tea bags and the enormous tin of Nescafé Blend

43. Fortunately, I had worked in public sector during one of the regular cost-saving purges and recognised such awful kitchen supplies. But then it didn't really matter, as I worked in the city and could nip out to buy a drinkable coffee from nearby café. There was no chance to do this here. I reluctantly chose a teabag and queued at the instant hot waterspout. There were a collection of sternly worded notices Blu-Tacked above the sink that threatened dire consequences if dirty teaspoons and mugs were left lying around.

I then opened the fridge to be greeted by a dairy of milk and an unbelievable number of Tupperware and old takeaway containers holding leftover food. There were so many containers wedged in there that it was as if someone from the maths department had organised it as a student display to try to illustrate a particularly tricky real-life mathematical problem. Post-it notes fluttered from some of the containers. As I closed the fridge I noticed the sign, in truly terrifying font, advising that EVERYTHING IN THIS FRIDGE WILL BE THROWN OUT AT THE END OF TERM 4. It was now Term 2. The staffroom fridge was a literal depiction of the teaching staff's daily intentions to eat a healthy lunch from home, and their obvious inability to do so.

Around me the teachers were catching up and grumbling about their workloads, troublemaking students and sports rosters. Just as I filled my mug with boiling water, the bell rang. I flinched, but managed not to burn myself, no doubt due to the subliminal messaging of the Health and Safety notices pinned above the sink. I put down my mug and found Mrs X who directed me to my final teacher. I followed the teacher into the next classroom, and sat again, trying to compose my face.

My next lesson after this was Assembly, where I sat next to Mrs X for comfort, while she issued general 'shushes' and 'quietly now' to the exuberant chatters. I somehow felt inhibited and wondered if I would ever be able to casually tell others (other than my children and husband of course) to be quiet. The world can be divided into two kinds of people: those who tell others to pick up rubbish, stop talking in the cinema and quieten down before the speeches (i.e. people who have the behavioural traits necessary for teaching) and those who just suffer fools in silence (inward seething optional). As I recoiled from the thought of telling unknown students to behave, I wondered again whether I was the kind of person who was made for teaching. The Assembly was just as mind- and bum-numbing as they had been when I was a student. Dust motes drifted slowly in the yellow light from the windows, even more languid and unrushed than the updates and thank you to the organising committee from the recent charity appeal. I then amused myself by trying to guess the sport or activity each student captained as they walked up to the microphone to announce their weekend results. It was obvious that by next week, I would have nothing to look forward to in Assembly, as all this suspense would be over.

After Assembly I sat through another history lesson taught by an energetic teacher with a devastatingly firm grasp on the details. In my last job, in the public sector, I'd been able to blather when I didn't know the answer, and then after a private period of hasty research and asking the nice man who sat at the next desk who had been in the department for ages, I could, at leisure, send a follow-up email with the information that was needed. Here the teacher confidently held forth, answered questions, and really knew her stuff. I'd been to university as an undergraduate nearly twenty years ago; I had pretty hazy memories of all of the content. Another knock to my confidence.

My next treat was lunchtime yard duty. Winter had almost arrived; the trees were bare and an icy breeze stirred up fallen leaves and empty chip packets. Some hardy students were sitting on the cold lawns, other older students clustered around the outside picnic tables while still others were running screaming and chasing each other through the yard. I walked solemnly backwards and forwards, as though I was a prison warden. I felt relief that there didn't seem to be anything serious to do. Our university lectures had regaled us with our legal duty of care when on yard duty, with firm instructions not to physically intervene to break up any fights. Fortunately, it didn't look as though there were going to be any fights. I milled around and wrestled with the usual dilemma about how to compose my face.

Halfway through lunch I was relieved by another teacher who had come for his yard duty, and he had sensibly bought a warm cup of tea with him. He asked if I had checked the classrooms. I hadn't. I actually had no idea what I was really meant do. I trailed behind him as he went into the nearest classroom block and chastised a group of lunching students, who had left food wrappers scattered on the classroom floor in such a determined fashion, complete with a decorative ring of mandarin skin on the floor around the classroom wastepaper basket, that it was like an art project. Finally, I summoned my inner strength, and did the most teacherly thing I could manage, and told the unknown students to pick up their rubbish. My confidence restored I then went off to the staffroom hoping to manage to eat my lunch in the ten minutes left.

By the time the final bell rang at 3.30 I was exhausted. The school emptied of students so quickly it was almost like a time-lapse film. In the staffroom, teachers either settled down at their desks to do some marking or grabbed whistles and First Aid kits and headed off to supervise school sport. I hightailed it out of the car park to collect my own children from their after-school care, and then headed home for my usual relaxing afternoon routine of listening to readers, cooking dinner and doing a load of laundry. After dinner, bath and the children's bedtime I realised that when I was a proper teacher, instead of surfing the internet or slumping in front of the television like a normal person, I would be marking and preparing my lessons for the next day.

I spent the rest of my first placement feeling sicker and sicker, under siege from a never-ending barrage of colds and viruses. If I missed one day of teaching placement there was no sensible indication of how I could make it up later in the year. The general feeling was that I had to soldier on. (I probably don't need to clarify that this was in the pre-Covid era, when airborne viruses were just another fun aspect of winter.) As I arrived, sneezing and apologetic in each classroom, my supervising teachers were all completely sympathetic. 'It happens to all new teachers,' they explained. 'Your immune system just isn't used to being exposed to so many different germs from the kids all the time. You will be continuously sick for the first year of teaching, but after that baptism of snot you will have a cast-iron constitution and only collapse when something really new like bird flu arrives.' I had a supervising teacher on my second placement who confirmed this and told me that after teaching for years she never got sick. My medical husband confirmed the same phenomenon was apparent in staff working at the Children's Hospital. 'Gastro all your first year,' he told me cheerfully, 'but then only the big guns get you as you have an immunity to most of the usual things.' So, for anyone contemplating becoming a teacher, just remember to factor in a full year of snot and high temperatures as part of your planning. So much of being a new teacher is intense and like a fever dream already, but feeling endlessly unwell amplifies the dislocating feeling of suddenly being a teacher.

I teach.
What's your
superpower?

5

MY GIFTED CHILD

My teaching has been predominantly in the private school sector. I try to be conscious of the privilege and unreality this involves, and also to avoid that most alumni of questions: 'Where did you go to school?' to find a familiar way to identify someone. Less than half of students in Australia are educated in the private sector, and while an examination of the results may not justify the cost, it's sometimes hard to see that when you are in the bubble of expensive gyms and lavish funding.

There are many features common to private schools. The most fascinating of these are private school mothers. They are (speaking treacherously here as one myself) a distinctive breed, hated by baristas across Australia. The stereotypical private school mother wears huge sunglasses at all times and in all weathers. The skinnier the mother, the bigger the sunglasses. The Queen Bee of the mothers at each school is the one that most closely resembles a bug.

The preferred hair colour is blonde, and author Liane Moriarty is completely on the money when she describes the blonde bobs. There are a lot of blonde bobs, all dead straight, regardless of the natural hair texture and colour. These blonde bobs are the ultimate achievement in manifestation. The sunglasses are possibly necessary because of the sparkle of the diamond stud earrings, or the shimmer from the shiny, spotless four-wheel drive SUVs that only go off road to mount a concrete kerb and nab a good park at the supermarket. The chosen shoes at school pick-up and drop-off are expensive sneakers, carefully coupled with designer activewear. Private school mothers are dressed to run a marathon at any time but are paradoxically unable to walk into the school gate from the car park. Instead, they like to park in loading bays, disabled car spots or just stop anywhere they like and activate their hazard lights (known as their 'park anywhere lights' in the trade). A friend likes to regularly send me photos from pick-up of the latest truly outrageously entitled park she has seen in the school car park.

Private school mothers can multitask and prove this twice a day when they arrive at school pick-up and drop-off holding both their iPhones and a takeaway coffee. When they flock together, the discussion is generally about how busy they are and, to be fair, the blondeness, the gym and the coffee do all take a lot of time. Some of them have inverted comma jobs, which are jobs that they have through their family or friends, and which enable them to take not only all school holidays off, but every family crisis day and, in fact, any day they fancy, just because. The inverted comma jobs also allow a lot of time for outrage, which is, as everyone knows, enormously time consuming as well. The outrage tends to focus on what their child has suffered, what the school has done now, and service quality of various baristas. There are, of course, lovely private school mothers who wear natural fibres to school pick-up, or who have non-inverted comma jobs, but as you never see them congregating at school (and barely hear from if you are a teacher), they are hardly part of this group.

As a teacher in the private school system I found that some of the private school mothers were one of the crosses I had to bear. (Of course, those teachers working in the Catholic sector can offer this up during prayer at Mass.) The students were almost all lovely, but sadly not all the mothers were as endearing. They would call the school and be surprised at not being able to immediately speak to you on the phone (yes that's right, I only teach your child and your child alone and I am sitting in an office thinking about how to best teach your child for the remainder of the day) and they sought continuous feedback on all results. They were concerned that you had either set too little homework or too much homework. The tasks were either too hard or far too easy. A subset of these mothers would take the year off from their inverted comma jobs when their child did Year 12 so that they could devote themselves tirelessly to badgering the teachers (and their child) for the whole year.

It is beyond a cliché to recognise that the progeny of these women were all gifted. Excessively gifted, even if conventional testing failed to accurately capture their talents. Tim Minchin's song 'Miracle' from *Matilda the Musical* accurately records the special nature of these children: 'one can hardly move for beauty and brilliance these days.' It was exhausting even contemplating where these unique abilities would carry them in the future, and how on earth their mothers would maintain the snow plough in front of their little darlings for the rest of their lives.

These mothers were of course the horrors, the unavoidable insects, but there were also many, many lovely private school parents I encountered during my time as a teacher. These were the ones who would give me a bottle of wine at the end of the year. No, I'm joking of course, these were really the ones who would give me a bottle of wine and a box of chocolates at the end of the year. Even those who did not give a gift were often charming. They were trying do their best. They loved their children and knew that they weren't perfect. They wanted the best for them and to help them to lead happy, productive lives. They had taught them manners. They had modelled compassion. They had taught their children that knowledge was important. They had tried to raise a good child. It was a pleasure to talk to them and we were united in our desire for their child to succeed in whatever it was they wanted to do, and for their child's missing school jumpers to be found.

As a school parent I was also struggling to fulfil the expectations on me. Once the novelty of my first placement had finished, I returned to the horror of struggling to get out of the house on time. Every weekday morning I had three external deadlines to meet – my youngest child's early learning centre, school for the oldest child and university for me – and my life became increasingly chaotic and frenzied. In the mornings my husband woke, went to the loo, showered, shaved, dressed, made two coffees (one for me and one in a travel cup for him), kissed us goodbye and then left the house. His life was as it ever was.

In a lament that I'm sure every mother will appreciate, by contrast, every weekday morning my routine went something like this:

- Wake up.
- Go to the loo.
- Wake the children.
- Feed the pets.
- Argue with children about the clothes they should wear that day.
- Look for daughter's missing shoe.
- Start preparing the wrong breakfasts for the children. Have ferocious argument with children about said breakfast, pointlessly stating things like, 'You liked it yesterday.'
- Start preparing the right breakfast for children.
- Keep looking for the missing shoe.
- Haul out yesterday's lunchboxes from kids' backpacks and mentally vow, as I do every morning, that tonight I really, really would empty and wash them so they would be sparkling and fresh for the next day.
- Tip the uneaten lunch and recess into the chook food bucket. Berate children for not eating their lunch and recess. Children reply they don't like the apples/pears/bananas they asked for yesterday.

• Cut my daughter's toast into fingers. She collapses, sobbing on the kitchen bench. I ask her what is wrong, in a tone that I hope expresses maternal care and love instead of deep frustration. Her reply, through theatrical sobs was: 'You know I hate toast in fingers.' Needless to say her triangular toast produced sobbing yesterday. I cut and tear the toast fingers into long triangles

• Urge my children, in a cross and ugly tone of voice, to eat up quickly as we are running late.

• Vow that tomorrow morning I will set my alarm earlier to avoid this stressful chaos.

• Nip outside to feed the chickens with the contents of the scrap bucket. The chickens cluck hello and rush to see me. They appreciatively literally rip into the food my children have rejected. I check for eggs and then return the house.

• Kiss my husband goodbye. I ask when we will see him tonight, and he says that he doesn't know.

• Unpack the dishwasher.

• Pack the dishwasher.

• Let the children get down from the bench and sadly note how there is more food on their plates after they have allegedly eaten breakfast then there was at the start of breakfast.

• Get children to start brushing their teeth.

• Send children out to look for their missing shoes.

• Shower and decide that I don't have time to wash my hair today. Resolve to get up earlier tomorrow.

• Spray dry shampoo in my hair for the third day

running. Realise is now nearly 50 per cent dry shampoo.

- Shout at the children to stop shouting at each other.
- Get dressed.
- Brush teeth and smear tinted sunscreen and lipstick on my face near where I hope it should go.
- Start packing children's bags and send my son to find his reader, which is lost somewhere in the house. Resolve that tonight I will pack everything up before I go to bed.
- Shout for children to put their shoes on immediately. My daughter emerges with only one shoe. Says she doesn't have any that match. I visit her bedroom and it is true, every other shoe she owns is missing. I ransack the house like a burglar on meth, upending cushions, crawling under furniture to look for the elusive shoe. I resolve that tonight I will ensure my children's footwear is all lined up in neat pairs before I go to bed.
- I shout and scream and rage about how late we are.
- I run around madly turning lights off and putting things back into the fridge.
- I decide that as my daughter's only pair of shoes that match are her little red gumboots, this is what she will wear to her early learning centre. She is delighted.
- I put children in the car, throw our bags in the boot and reverse at speed from the garage.
- A hideous scraping noise alerts me to the fact that I have run over one of my children's bicycles. Again. I resolve that tonight I will make sure the bicycles are put away neatly in the shed before I go to bed.
- I drive to the early learning centre trying to make

loving conversation and not feel resentful because I can't hear the news and the weather on the radio.

• My daughter discovers one of her missing shoes is in the car (its pair is still sadly at home). I ask her why the shoe was in the car. She says because it was full of sand from the sandpit, and then turns the shoe upside down to demonstrate, pouring sand all over her brother who gets some in his eye and starts crying.

• I take both children into my daughter's early learning centre and sign her in and remember that we didn't bring in the specific thing we were meant to bring in for today's special 'Make Mummy Feel Inadequate Day'. I resolve that tonight I will write the chore for the next 'Make Mummy Feel Inadequate Day' on the kitchen calendar, and then look at the calendar calmly every morning during our relaxing and nurturing breakfast.

• I return to the car with just my son and drive him to school. The car park is full and as we are walking towards the school gates I notice a glamorous, gym-gear-wearing mother with a full face of makeup and a bouncy blow dry happily pulling into the handy disabled park and retrieving a schoolbag from her spotlessly clean car boot. My son, who has a keen sense of justice and an equally keen carrying voice, asks in a tone of outrage: 'Why is that mummy parking in the disabled park?' I reply that the poor mummy is disabled as she can't read, and then realise that the poor mummy has silently and swiftly moved into earshot thanks to her luxury sneakers, and I smile cravenly at her as she walks angrily past. I wonder if maybe the camel toe in her running leggings is, in fact, a disability worthy of a special car park.

• I escort my son to his classroom and then return to my car, power walking so I can leave the car park before it sets solid with the before-work traffic.

• I finally drive, alone, to university. I park and gallop to my first lecture.

I now understand why the mature-aged women in my undergraduate classes were less than amused when I'd failed to prepare for a tutorial because 'I'd slept in'. Frankly, I don't know why they didn't just slap me. Their take-no-prisoners attitude is now more understandable, as I too had my tolerance stocks depleted by 9am.

After such a relaxing morning routine, I feel exhausted and ready to return home to bed. But instead, I dutifully file into my first lecture, ready to listen to professors speak about the importance of nurturing dialogue and a calm learning environment, which I hoped that my children were getting at their schools.

Let's eat grandma.
Let's eat, Grandma.
Punctuation
saves lives.

6

IS THIS GOING TOWARDS OUR MARKS?

I spent most of my time at university being coached in how to teach senior English, which involved drawing up a unit of work and four weeks' worth of lesson plans for teaching one of the components of the English course. The lecturer explained that having such a well-prepared unit plan up our sleeves will be invaluable when we eventually start to teach.

I had decided to teach a fabulous novel I love, Kate Grenville's *The Secret River*, for this theoretical unit and all I needed to do, having read the book already, was interpret the curriculum documents and use them to create lessons that would result in students who could produce an essay or written assignment that would meet the higher marking criteria. I opened the curriculum documents online. These were written in a dense jargon that tortured every sentence and obscured all meaning. The fact that this had been written by English teachers for English teachers was an exquisite irony I did not have time to appreciate right then.

Instead, I started pondering what were some aspects of culture in the novel, and how I could encourage students to consider these cultural perspective in the text. My teaching had to meet the curriculum requirements, and students' understanding of texts were filtered through the lens of language and stylistic features, and context. In my own Jurassic past, when studying English, the word 'feature' had never featured. I remember lots of writing about the themes being explored by the writer. It seemed simpler, and in a nostalgic way, more enjoyable. I was qualified to teach English because I held a Bachelor of Arts degree majoring in English. Basically, I spent three years on a whistle-stop tour through English literature from Beowulf to Tom Stoppard. My undergraduate university was a new red-brick one, built around a lake (which I was delighted to discover, when living in the UK, followed the building plan of all English red-brick universities, meaning that I could easily find the tavern on any post World War Two English campus). My university had radically and counter-culturally decided in the 1990s to teach a narrative-led, chronologically oriented English course primarily guided by the hefty two-volume *Norton Anthology of English Literature*. Volume one had a cover with a picture of Queen Elizabeth I looking exactly like Miranda Richardson in *Blackadder*, and volume two had a blurry Turner landscape on the cover, which suggested that he suffered from myopia almost as badly as I did. I lugged at least one of these volumes to campus every day I had to be there (i.e. three arduous days a week), and spent hours flicking through the dense type and thin rice paper pages. As someone who fondly remembered the good nougat that used to appear at dinner parties, the kind wrapped in the miraculously edible rice paper, that was 'for the adults', I have a residual Proustian memory about any thin translucent paper and tended to lick my fingers a lot while I was studying.

As we progressed through the evolution of English literature I enjoyed taking classes in medieval literature, Swiftian satire and the development of the novel. I had been at school during the 'whole language' era in 1980s and had never properly studied a foreign language, which meant that I had missed out on learning about grammar. My university English course avoided grammar too, so as a teacher I had to read the school grammar textbooks to find out what I was meant to know.

I remain unconvinced that senior school students are best served by being compelled to review texts through the prism of whatever critical theory was fashionable ten years ago when the curriculum-writing teachers were being trained.

In a reactionary way, I think that parents, students, employers and even – I'm bringing out the big guns here – society (but I accept that you may not believe in society, even if it believes in you), think that English classes at school should focus on producing adults who can read, write clearly, spell reasonably accurately when there is no spellcheck available, and be able to apply basic grammatical rules to their writing. (I don't give a stuff about the pedantic rules like those against split infinitives, which still survive because Boomers crave irritation.) Senior school students should also be taught how to write an essay, deliver a speech, understand persuasion, know how poems, plays, novels and films are constructed and be able to analyse them. They should also have at least a nodding acquaintance with the Western cannon of literature, plus some of the works of the oppressed: Australians, espeically Indigenous Australians, and female authors. It would also be ideal if students left school with an enjoyment of literature and a love of reading, but I'd settle for even a vaguely positive feeling about reading for pleasure. My views are not shared by those who write the English curricula in Australia.

I think that I am especially sceptical of modern trends in educational theory in teaching English as I was at my local South Australian primary school in the 1980s, when the truly radical trends of the 1970s were being implemented (as always, ten years after they were fashionable at universities). As a result, I did not have to do any work if I did not want to. Unsurprisingly, as a child (and in fact as part of my adult personality as well), I often did not want to. If I wanted to read a *Babysitters Club* book quietly by myself all day on the mustard yellow corduroy beanbag in the classroom corner, I could do that (as fortunately my mother had taught me to read before I went to school). I did not have to do maths, and to this day am unsure about where to put the remainder when I subtract. I did enjoy art and craft and spent hours making ashtrays and glazing them in readiness for the kiln, although macramé was far too methodical so I never learned to do that either. My parents finally rebelled against my extensive primary school training as a potter and consumer of *Babysitter*

Club stories. They hung onto our second-hand Valiant station wagon for fifteen more years, spent nothing on technology, travel or fashion, to send me to a private school that they hoped would teach the unfashionable basics. It was a choice they were lucky to have, but I believe that every student should be able to attend a good school and, ideally, the local school should be that good school

There was however, one break in the relaxed hippy vibe of colourful skivvies and cords that was my primary schooling in 1980s South Australia, when we moved to Queensland for a year, and I went to a new local school. Queensland in the 1980s was at the height of the Bjelke-Petersen era. It was the 1950s still in Queensland. It's not often that you leave South Australia and feel smug and ahead of the game but heading North with the bananas did unleash all of that and then some. In my Queensland school the name of the state was obvious, as there was a framed picture of the Queen on the wall of the classroom, as well as on every spare wall of the school. There was corporal punishment within the walls of the classroom. There were unfeeling teachers who didn't let me go to the toilet when I needed to go, and who then humiliated me when I wet my pants, proving that I was right and I did, in fact, need to leave the classroom. There was a flag-saluting ceremony in the morning under the burning hot sun while we were lined up in separate boy and girl lines on the bitumen. We sang 'God Save the Queen'. I wasn't allowed to wear a hat during these patriotic proceedings, even though clearly the Queen, should she have come to our school, would have been able to wear hers. Being made to stay hatless especially rankled because I was a girl and theoretically was (according to my mother) even allowed to wear a hat inside. My hatless time outside meant I got more sunburnt and freckled every day. Maybe it was part of the school's plan to provide physical damage to pair with the psychological damage they were inflicting. Despite it being a state school, there were also religious education classes, where I was surprised to discover that I was a member of the Church of England. I coloured in pictures of Bible stories during these lessons. There was grammar. There was homework. There was a hot classroom on stilts, and clothes pegs put on the tongues of boys (but not girls) who talked too much. Eventually, as I was such a dangerous chatterbox, no boy would willingly sit next to me. (This has continued throughout life.) I ended this year with a terror of Queenslanders. My parents ended this year with mixed feelings. They were cross about my school experience in the Queensland educational system but would lyrically recall the homework and the rigour whenever they reflected on my soft, southern, primary school. This was, I suppose, an immersion in a system that was not following educational trends. It was a terrifying experience and gave me a valuable insight into how powerless and scared a school student can feel.

My university studies were trying to marinate me in current educational theory. Or at least, given the speed of the course, give me quick sprinkle with the essentials. I was, thanks to my own varied history of being exposed to educational theory, a little wary of the latest trends. Like the true Australian I am, I feel uneasy with 'isms', but very reassured by 'the vibe'. The experience of teachers and the reality of classroom practice is often disregraded by a new theory imposed from high. Anyone who has taught or been taught in a corner of noisy open plan classrooms knows how disapointing other people's theories can be.

I spent my studies writing essays on current theories about how to teach and drafting the little knowledge I had into preparing lessons I could teach when I was finally unleashed on my own classes. I felt uneasy that I wasn't doing it right, that I was obtusely failing to understand what was expected of me. I hoped that when I was out in front of my own class, it would make more sense.

I'm a maths
teacher.
Of course
I've got
problems.

7

PLEASE SIR, MAY I HAVE A JOB?

It proved hugely difficult for me to land a contract as a teaching graduate, as my failure to synchronise my life stages with the global economy continued, in true Gen X fashion. The recent crash in the stock market and the global financial crisis meant that no old teacher could afford to retire, and the tsunami of recent graduates of teaching from universities pumping them out meant that there was fierce hand-to-hand combat for good jobs. Most teaching posts weren't advertised but simply tossed to the familiar starving substitute teachers hanging around the school, as keenly hungry for a permanent job as stray dogs gathering near the butchers for scraps.

I'd left university the first time in the depths of the 1990s recession, where most graduates rushed overseas (London or Hong Kong) to find a job. It had been so disheartening looking for work as a new lawyer then. Now I could not believe that I was again newly qualified in a different profession that also had a surplus of graduates. Online forums were filled with nightmare stories of teachers who could not find full-time work, part-time work or get a mortgage.

I had been awarded a prize for being a high achiever in my year at university, a prize which was calculated on our academic marks and our placement reports from the schools where we had done our on-the-job teacher training.

I had hoped, with this shining endorsement in my pocket, along with the fact that I was old(er), had done well at school in my Year 12 exams a million years ago, had a good academic record at university, and was an experienced and proven worker, might make it easier for me to stand out from the crowd.

It did not impress the Department of Education. I spent hours online filling in forms, and said I was willing to teach English at any school within 200 kilometres of my house, under any sort of contract. I received zero offers to teach, or even to relief teach. I was so surprised, and so naïve, that I telephoned the Department to ask whether something had gone wrong. Perhaps my application had not been received? The woman I reached on the phone looked up my details and confirmed that I was properly registered on the system.

'But I haven't had a single offer,' I complained. 'Not even for one half day of relief-teaching.'

'There are lots of graduates,' she said.

'I know,' I replied. 'I've just been at uni with them all. But surely you must need at least some new teachers?'

'We'll be in touch if something opens up,' she said, and ended the call.

I dutifully updated my details with the Department of Education next year as well and did not receive so much as a fart in my general direction. After their resounding personal rejection of me, I started applying for jobs in the private school system, which was prepared to overlook my manifest deficiencies and offer me work.

I then spent a year struggling through a succession of relief contracts of various dubious matches to my skill set. Relief-teaching, for those who don't know, is what the Americans call substitute teaching. You hang around at home every morning to see if disaster has struck a regular teacher so you can come in and take their lessons. You are 'relieving' another teacher of their class, or maybe providing some 'relief' to their students. Short-term contracts are a step further where you cover a teacher for a planned period, such as a term while they take their long service leave or a six-week stint after an operation.

Graduate teachers are, in general, regarded as a liability as teachers but blessedly cheap and a good deal for a school that is already paying a regular teacher and just needs to get a fill-in. This is actually fair. I learnt more from these experiences as a grass-green teacher than my students ever did. These varied contracts enabled me to gain a practical grounding in teaching pedagogy. (That might be the most teacher-training-influenced sentence I have ever written.)

My new teacher skills included never using the word 'pedagogy' except in a letter of application for a teaching position, how to look up answers online or in the back of the textbook during a lesson without the class noticing, carrying marking everywhere so that I could always take the opportunity to do some if ever I got to sit down, and how to subtly convince the most annoying student in the class to spend an hour in the sick bay with the school nurse so everyone else could have some peace. I'd also, and most importantly, been able to work on my hard stare (modelled on Paddington Bear's hard stare) to subdue off-task behaviour, and to ask students to keep sitting down at the end of the day after the bell rang, because 'the bell doesn't dismiss you, I do.'

I'd also learnt some valuable practical knowledge during my year of relief-teaching: that the teacher librarian and the staff member who allocated relief lessons are the two people you should assiduously cultivate, as they will be able to help you out of almost any pickle. I'd also realised that for English teachers, marking is an avalanche that will smother you alive if you ever stop running. Other hard-won knowledge was to never take a job at a school that doesn't have a cluster of shops nearby or you will instantly become trapped on campus and forced to eat canteen food exactly like you are a student yourself. Finally, and most importantly, never willingly take a relief drama lesson as you will have twenty-five students raucously roaming the campus to 'rehearse', or, even worse, you will have to sit through a whole lot of awful performances. (Just kidding, I love to watch you all emote! Seriously, it's so inspiring! You are so much better at the end of the lesson now after your rehearsing! And no, I would never say these things to another class! You are all the best!)

I'd also gained many painful personal insights from my relief-teaching. The key one was, not unsurprisingly, as the owner of a succession of poorly behaved cats, dogs and children, that I am not very good at maintaining discipline and keeping a quiet classroom. I tended to be amused by mildly bad behaviour and outrageous student lies and had an unfortunate inability to take everything seriously. Teachers are required to be po-faced about so many things, and some days you just don't have enough grump to give.

There is a lot that is good about relief-teaching, and many teachers deliberately decide to make it their career. Relief-teachers receive a higher hourly pay rate (to compensate for their lack of sick pay), seldom have to write reports or attend parent–teacher interviews, can take holidays during term time and don't have to spend every day locked up with a class they hate. But I still wanted my own class, one I could teach all year and mould as my own. A group I could even call 'my class' as opposed to 'Mrs Healey on stress leave's' class.

After a succession of horrific job interviews, where I again displayed nothing but my deeply innate ability to say the wrong things at the wrong time, I finally interviewed at a school I liked, with teachers and a management team who seemed friendly and interested in the same kinds of things I was. Their management included some other teachers who had moved into education after working in other spheres, and so they understood why and how I was thirty-nine and had only a year of teaching experience. We spent most of my interview laughing about the improvements needed in the Graduate Diploma of Education and talking about plays we had seen recently. It was heaven. English teacher heaven, but there you go.

As a side note about English teacher heaven, a divine vision that I feel compelled to linger over, it would be a low-key, restrained sort of celestial environment. Not a flashy Valhalla. In fact, for the non-English teachers it might even seem a bit hellish. There would also be excellent hot coffee, magical marking piles that vanished once you had started (like a reverse Magic Pudding), classes that worked silently but were also capable of sustaining insightful classroom discussions whenever you asked a question, congenial colleagues, no reports, no sports days, no sport or drama commitments unless you had once been on the national soccer team and just loved your sport, students who arrived on Monday morning just itching to tell you all about the great book they read over the weekend, highbrow chat about books, telly and movies all day plus students who steadily improved through the year and who read and took action regarding the comments you had made when marking their work. There would also be a small scattering of grammatical errors, misplaced apostrophes and inadvertent puns every day, so that the English teachers could feel smug and happy pointing them out. Small imperfections are needed for true perfection.

I was offered my own class (six of them in fact) with a full-time load. I was even offered two Year 9 classes. After a year of contract and relief-teaching I knew exactly why the new teacher would get two Year 9 classes. Year 9 is generally agreed to be the worst year for even the best of students. A clash of puberty, peer pressure and brain development combine to make the students almost unteachable. Geelong Grammar (where Prince Charles did some time) deal with this by sending Year 9 students away to another campus – Timbertop – for the whole year, where the students can do outdoor activities and get it all out of their system. In most other schools, where Year 9s have to be on campus, they are kept from the good teachers, in case they cause them to lose their mojo. The Year 9s are dealt out to the new and inexperienced teachers. Even with double Year 9, a job was a job, and I happily agreed. I was filled with enthusiasm, drive and was certain that this job would bring me the balance and meaning in life I had been dreaming of.

I proudly signed my first proper teaching contract in December. Understandably, schools like to go into the summer holidays prepared for the year ahead and so the head of English e-mailed me to say welcoming things and attached a list of texts I would be covering in Term 1, as well as a description of the texts I still had to choose. I sent a few emails back but when there was no response, it became clear that although the teachers were well meaning they were also flat to the floor. Once school holidays began, I received an email advising that I could sort out the details in mid-January when we came back to school.

Mid-January? But my own children didn't go back to school until the very end of January. My fabled holidays started to shrink. I would have been more worried about this if I hadn't had so much reading to do. I would be teaching a Shakespeare play that I had somehow managed to escape reading at school or university, plus a stack of novels, plays and short stories I'd never read before. I moaned and moaned about the selections, then started reading and re-reading, taking notes and writing lists of possible activities and creating some lesson plans. It took weeks. I was also struggling to find texts I wanted to teach. They had to be suitable for teenagers, well written, contain oodles of literary techniques for class dissection, be interesting, not too long and engaging enough to withstand weeks of scrutiny. I learnt again that it is much easier to bitch about someone else's choice than it is to make your own choice.

We went on our annual summer pilgrimage to the beach, and this time I had a new stack of books to take and fail to read. A friend came by and saw me lying in bed (my natural habitat) and recoiled in horror at the pile of Shakespeare on the bedside table. I live in my nightie all summer holidays, which is actually entirely practical when you need to be ready for a nap at any time, and your drab fashion sense (and ample bust) incline you towards all cotton flowing mumsy nighties rather than sexy satin.

'You can't be reading that?' she squealed, like it was hardcore porn or *Mein Kampf*.

'No, I'm not,' I said soothingly. 'I am meant to be reading it.' I waved my arm in an airy fashion, and an old, dog-eared copy of Jilly Cooper's *Rivals*, a book I re-read at every idle moment and was actually reading instead, fell comfortingly on the floor.

'But why?'

'Teaching.'

'Nothing would make me read Shakespeare,' she said firmly. 'Nothing at all.'

We returned from my final 'normal' summer holiday, where my joy at finally becoming a proper teacher had only been slightly clouded by my failure to do the work required to be a proper teacher.

I'm the awesome
science teacher
everyone's
talking
about.

8

PRIOR PREPARATION PREVENTS POOR PERFORMANCE ... POSSIBLY

My first week as a proper on-the-books, real teacher was spent at my new school, during the end of the summer holidays, planning lessons, attending professional development sessions and going to meetings. Planning a year's work for each class is a careful juggle, as you look over the curriculum and the mandatory tasks, and in English classes, try to fill five lessons a week, for forty weeks of term time. If I wasn't an English teacher, I could tell you how many lessons that is. It's a lot.

Lesson planning involves thinking wildly optimistic thoughts about how quickly your class will read a novel, and then trying to think of an assessment task that will capture some of the mandatory competencies without being too boring, and which will allow a spread of activities and skills. You then can produce all sorts of charts and programs that list these deadlines, and actually (if you are organised) write out the task sheets and the marking criteria for each task. If you are really on fire, you can also create the formative activities and their resources, and plan out how you will teach each lesson. When you are a new teacher, this seems a huge mountain, a rocky Everest of work. It takes forever, partly because you have to keep checking the ropes and seeing where others have gone before. Experienced teachers won't have to re-do all of this work every year and can often just roll their previous year's work over, tweaking the bits that were dull or the students didn't understand.

Occasionally, of course, the curriculum is revised, a truly horrible time that is usually foreshadowed by years of right-wing whingeing in newspaper opinion pieces about the downgrading of educational standards and the imposition of the black armband view of history on students. (It is history that gets everyone the most fired up. Somehow, we can all agree that learning the sequence of English Kings and Queens is not what Australian school children need but can't agree on more than that.) There is usually a curriculum revamp after a change in government, as, just like renaming government departments, incumbents like to put their stamp on things, and some differences makes it harder to make comparisons and assess whether new policies and initiatives are working.

My school gave us until the fourth week of the school year to complete all this planning, and then everything, including all the tasks, had to be uploaded onto a central database so that it could be checked and then made available to the students. The plans for Year 11 and 12 students also needed to be completed on an approved form and then submitted to the relevant state education body for review.

In my laughably small files, I had one 'unit' of work, teacher-speak for about four weeks' worth of planned lessons and activities for one class, along with the summative assessment task. This was the task I had prepared at university for an assignment, my novel study of Kate Grenville's *The Secret River*. I had been relying on this. However, my boss, the head of the English faculty, told me that students hated this novel and strongly recommended that I did not teach it. This meant that I had no work prepared for any of my six classes. I tried not to get too stressed about the amount of work I needed to do, and just knuckle down and do it. I stayed up every night until 1am for three weeks straight trying to get the planning done, and spent all weekend hunched over my laptop, discretely flicking through textbooks and the teacher's copies of my chosen novels, inserting Post-it notes and scribbling other notes to myself. I have since discovered that the State Education Department does protect new teachers a bit by not giving them a full teaching load (i.e. giving them only four or five classes) for their first year, so that the planning load doesn't kill them. The private schools take their pound of flesh or, more likely, expect that you have been blooded in a public sector school.

In the first week of the school year, when the teachers are back but the students aren't, the school campus looks immaculate, reminiscent of the *Yes Minister* episode about the model hospital that was perfect because it had no patients. The campus gardens are filled with flowers and enthusiastic ground staff mowing and mulching. School garden beds, much like school itself, are invariably ruined and look disgusting once balls appear.

The teaching staff are also relaxed before the students arrive back on campus. There is lots of chat and cheerful catch-up. The staff have tans, freshly dyed hair and calm, fresh faces, unrecognisable from the haggard, grey-haired specimens who were frantically marking when you saw them at the end of the previous year. Teachers, especially senior school teachers, are a bit like football club coaches. Their successes are measured by the success of the team they have been dealt. You can inspire them, you can encourage them and you can even teach them, but in the end, it's really hard to achieve greatness when you are dealt a bad hand. (Like Kenny Rogers croons, you've got to know when to hold them, when to fold them, and when to run. Plenty of good teachers have fled their school or even the profession altogether back to the safety of the office when they were dealt the 'run' class.) Success is, of course, relative and in some years and some contexts, just getting your students over the line, or even near the line, is also a triumph worth celebrating. What success looks like is different for every student and for every class. Failure is also surprisingly individualistic too.

The upside of this is, however, that the brilliant results of your students are also ascribed to you. Sometimes a fabulously gifted student arrives in class, with a much higher IQ and far better read than you and, like a gift from the gods, already able to use apostrophes appropriately. Then you can just sit back, talk novels and authors with them while the rest of the class labours away in the background and you try not to say 'later, this is actually interesting,' too often to the other students in the room. Following the completion of the exam season, you can falsely and modestly accept the plaudits in the staffroom after the Year 12 results come out. So, the planning week also has a few staff happily saying 'it was nothing' as they cruise the staffrooms.

Even though as a newbie I was desperate to get my lesson planning finished, the first week of the school year (week 0) is also filled with meetings that stretch on and on. Teaching management love meetings. Meetings are like cocktail parties, you don't want to go, but you are cross not to be asked. Meetings are assemblies for grown-ups, they go on for far too long, and always involve a droner who holds the floor for hours. The only good thing about a meeting is that it lets you do those pelvic floor exercises you never otherwise have time for. Once you've flexed those muscles into submission, you can then play 'meeting Bingo' and record how many times management use the latest jargon, usually something like 'reaching out', 'capabilities' or 'enrichment.'

My first official meeting for the teachers was enlightening. We were given an inspiring pep talk by the Principal and the Vice Principal and then handed our class lists. These are one of the most important documents that shape your teaching year or semester. Like much else as a teacher, you can't control them, instead, 'you get what you get and you don't get upset'. The class lists are the confirmation of exactly what subjects, what year levels you will be teaching, and, crucially, the names of the twenty-five students who will be in each class.

Once you have been at school for a while and know the

students, you can scan through the lists and see who the fates (and the timetable at the school) have pre-destined for your year. You feel a warm glow when you see the names of lovely students you have taught previously and, it must be admitted, sense a sinking feeling in the pit of your stomach when you see other names. In the same way that you just can't gel with everyone you meet, in the case of some kids, there is what people sometimes describe as a 'personality clash'. All you can do is hope that you get dealt a good hand, with more good cards than bad. Reviewing the class list is also that moment when, exactly as everyone who has ever had an older sibling at their school suspected anyway, teachers look at familiar surnames and wonder if the younger child will be like the older one.

We were then handed details of the students in our classes with special needs. Pages and pages. A book almost. I joked that maybe we could just have the list of those students without special needs, but this banter fell on stony ground. There were psychologists' reports everywhere. I kept hearing that other people were training to be psychologists, and now I knew why. Of course, one of the things that parents hope that private schooling will provide for their students is extra help, and parents shell out the big bucks in the hope that their children will receive this help. There were also students who were dealing with personal tragedies (mainly inflicted by the familiar characters of illness, death and conflict).

The students in my charge had been diagnosed with anxiety, depression, eating disorders, sleep disorders, ADHD, conflict disorders, and hearing and/or vison impairments, and some were recovering from surgery, battling Epstein-Barr viruses or recovering from childhood cancers. Some of them had even been diagnosed with the more education-based learning disorders, dyslexia, dysgraphia or dyscalculia, and I felt overwhelmed. I could dimly remember one lecture at university about teaching students with special needs. Occasionally lecturers had mentioned the need to provide information in more than one manner, so as to capture different learning styles.

I had been prepared to teach the average students. I had no idea how to deal with these disorders. I had no idea what some of these disorders even were. I had no idea how to modify my lessons or my teaching style to best accommodate these students. I had wanted to teach, and now it seemed that I needed to offer so much more. I felt uneasy, as the first hint of my epic ignorance began to slowly move through my sluggish brain, like the tiny zephyr that arrives before a hurricane.

Our leader charged on, mentioning guidance notes and learning plans that had been developed for each of these students. While he kept talking, I desperately flicked to the plans. They suggested tailored lessons and tailored tasks. Basically, they meant more work for me, and demanded skills that I did not have. My own anxiety levels were rising. When we were offered our first tea break (teachers might love meetings but they fortunately love recess breaks too), I carefully herded my supervising teacher out of the group, where she had been happily gossiping and having a cup of tea (quintessential teacher activities).

'My form list,' I said, 'I'm freaking out.' (Now that my job as an English teacher was in the bag, I had resorted to my usual colloquial language.)

'You'll be fine,' she said, her eyes not meeting mine and instead following a new platter of cakes that had arrived from the school canteen and were being handed around. 'Every new teacher thinks they won't be able to cope. You'll be fine.'

'Or you'll have a breakdown,' interjected a man in shorts and sneakers, with an irritating faux jolly manner that tried, and failed, to mask basic cruelty. Correctly deducing that he was a PE teacher and therefore had nothing to offer me unless I needed to learn the rules of softball, I glared at him. Being six feet tall has its downsides when it comes to sitting in planes, the back seats of cars and buying jumpsuits, but is absolutely fabulous for getting things down from high shelves, seeing the stage at concerts and glaring at people in an intimidating way. I blasted my most imperious look at him straight down my nose.

He muttered a resentful, 'I'm just joking,' and sprang away on his irritatingly muscly legs.

My supervisor made a sudden dive at the passing platter of cakes and then, treat in hand, turned to face me properly.

'Georgie,' she said. 'Stop worrying. Put your tasks on the school's learning system so that the kids' parents and tutors can see them too. For every task, talk about it, chalk about it and have a printed handout. Organise modified tasks for the kids with special needs. If you have a class that is particularly at risk, be careful to select appropriate texts. You seem like you actually give a shit, and that will put you ahead of the pack. For the Year 11s and 12s, just talk to the school's special education supervisor, as absolutely everything can be modified. Relax.'

'Can we do some professional development on special needs?' I asked, having swallowed my calming slab of cake, but not all my anxiety.

'There'll be something on autism and dyslexia scheduled already – we do autism and dyslexia every year.' She looked intently at me. 'Relax. You will be fine. Remember, you are the teacher.'

'That's what I'm frightened of,' I said, trying and failing to make it sound like a joke.

'I'll see you in the faculty meeting.'

Our English faculty meetings were, unexpectedly, a delight. The head of the faculty arranged food for us again (who doesn't love a meeting with food) and we had a peaceful talk about our own summer reading before we settled down to the business of scheduling moderated marking, mid-year exams, the school's policy on draft copies of work and the planned excursions for the year. I tried and failed to remember all the names of the English teachers, and then collected my children, went home, and determinedly sat at the kitchen table for even more planning.

Sadly, the first proper day of school arrived. I realised, belatedly and stupidly, that teachers don't get to walk their own children into school on the first day. Feeling incredibly guilty about missing this key milestone, I dropped my children off at before school care, and then raced to work. The work–life balance was booming again, as I realised that I also wouldn't be there for pick-up. Teachers get great holidays, but it's almost impossible to do anything during school term as, understandably, you are paid to be at school for the academic year. Not being on site costs the school money, as they have to hire a relief-teacher to take your classes for the day.

Normal people, in normal jobs, who don't have bells ring to end their lunchtime, and who don't have to pick up rubbish on their way to work, usually get four weeks of annual leave a year. Teachers get twelve weeks of leave. Four of these (usually the last week of every holiday) will always be filled with marking and lesson preparation, and if you teach a senior 'language-rich' subject like English, history or geography, then about double this, so at least eight weeks of non-term time over the year will be filled with marking and lesson preparation. If you teach primary school, then there is obviously less marking, but there are also a lot of small children, screaming, untied shoelaces and snot in your working hours.

Teachers who are parents are also able to cope with the twelve weeks of holidays that their own children get and so manage, unlike all other types of parents, to cover the school holiday situation without going broke. Even though teachers do get holidays (which are fabulous, I won't deny, and which never get cancelled for the usual crap reasons they do in other industries like too many orders, too busy, too many people sick or your supervisor has already booked a ski holiday then), there is a downside. Of course. The most obvious is that your holidays are fixed and you will travel in the busy season with all the other children in the nation and the peak prices until you retire.

Another downside of the inflexibility is that (like others with real jobs at a coalface, literal or otherwise) unless you teach your child's own class or in their section of the school, you won't get to pick up or drop off your own kid at school and chat to their teacher. Instead, you'll be having stressful chats with your own students' parents. You will never see your own child perform in school assembly or pick up an award. (In all honesty, this might never happen anyway, but it's still a fabulous mum-guilt grievance to ruminate over on a sleepless night.) You will never see a sports day or a swimming carnival (this piece of news might actually encourage some to become teachers so I'm just putting it out there).

On my son's first school sports day I had a temporary teaching contract that was only part-time, so after teaching a few lessons I drove to his school to be supportive and watch him in his events. I finally found him and gave him a wave. (The first rule of parenting, as in so much else in life, is if you are not seen and publicly acknowledged to be doing something, then you may as well not have done it.) He saw me, beamed and ran towards me, his sun-safe sports hat flapping in the breeze.

'Mummy, you're here.'

'I've been watching you for ages,' I lied. 'You have been doing so well.'

'It's so good you're here,' he continued. 'Can we go home now? I have had enough.'

'But sports day isn't over yet darling,' I said, to the amusement of the other parents watching this development from the sidelines. The literal sidelines. 'It goes on all day.'

'No,' he groaned. 'But I guess then it will be done and I will never have to do it again.'

'It happens every year,' I said brightly. 'So only twelve more sports days to go, and then you are done.' (As parents know, if a line amuses you, run with it. You have to take your pleasure where you can find it. Your kids will only laugh at your jokes when you put a chip up each nostril and pretend to be a walrus, so you need to make your own fun and then laugh at your own jokes.)

This bought out a bit of murmuring from the sidelines. Judging other parents is another key parental function, and many of the spectators, particularly the lycra- and sneaker-clad women who wanted to advertise that they had already been for a run that day, and that yes, their camel toe was pretty impressive, obviously disapproved of my attitude. Sports day was fun. Making children race against each other for colourful ribbons was healthy. Ranking children publicly for their talents, something that hadn't been allowed in a classroom for twenty years (back when corporal punishment was still a weapon in a teacher's arsenal) was a great idea when it happened outside an oval in front of their peers and strange adults. The murmuring disapproval grew louder. One of the mothers, the sort who 'spoke through her child' for maximum passive aggressiveness and annoyance, spoke up, ostensibly to her child, who had drifted close to our group once his event was over. He was clutching a new blue ribbon in his hand.

'Now, little Johnny,' she said, looking at her child, but using the kind of carrying voice that she probably used to summon her dog home from a neighbouring suburb. 'We love sports day, don't we? A positive attitude is so important, isn't it? Sports day is fun, isn't it Johnny?'

A positive murmur of assent swept the crowd. The un-Australian sports hater, and negligent mother who didn't even bother to be supportive for the whole sports day, was being put in her place. I could not bear it. Two could play at this game.

'Well darling,' I said, in my own carrying voice. 'It isn't really that bad. Sports day lets all the little children who are no good in the classroom have their chance to shine. It's a special day for them. And that's nice for them too.' My son, unsurprisingly, had no response to this comment, and stood silently, breathing through his open mouth. Ideally, I would have swept out of the school right then, with a swish of my *Dynasty*-style pleated skirt, but instead of course hung around for another half an hour, in my crumpled daggy clothes, shunned by the other mothers at the coffee caravan. So actually, my time at sports day was pretty much like every other school event I attended.

At my own school, on the big first day, I collected my new name tag (which made me feel like I was working at a fast-food restaurant again) and a map of the campus. I dropped my bags off to my allocated desk in the workroom – as the new employee I had of course been assigned a desk cunningly just between the printer and the toilets – and I had that vital last wee to tide me over for the day. When I reached my new homeroom, I found about forty kids sitting on chairs, lounging against walls and chatting like they were at a cocktail party. I had to clear a group of students off my desk so I could sit down.

'Hi,' I said. 'I'm your new teacher. Mrs Brooks.'

One nearby boy, who wasn't actually speaking, looked blankly at me and then looked away. No-one else paid me any attention at all. A propitious start. Embarrassed, I opened my laptop and tried to work out if I had been sent to cover another teacher as a 'relief' in my one free lesson for today. No, thank goodness. Everyone was, unsurprisingly really, available to teach their allocated lessons on the first day back.

I then thoroughly looked around, trying to match faces to the class list complete with mug shots from student ID cards that I had been sent last year. Except for the red-haired twins (who I had already accepted I would not be able to differentiate for the entire year) I could not recognise a soul. Teenagers change so fast that school photos taken a year ago can only ever be the roughest guide to identity. It's a bit like driving into Melbourne or Sydney on the new freeways, using your old *Road Atlas of Australia*, the one with a 1970s Holden and a groovy couple wearing flares on the front cover. Finally, when I could not have been ignored any longer or more determinedly, the bell rang and a good portion of the students mooched outside, without giving me a second glance. Once the visitors had left, I introduced myself again, organised everyone into seats and started to take the roll and run through the daily notices.

Outside, in a cunningly orchestrated manoeuvre, the school groundskeepers had fired up a leaf blower, so I had to strain to make myself heard. I was to find, over the course of the year, that the leaf blowers would blare through roll call every day, regardless of the season. By March, as a result of projecting my voice to compete with the leaf blowers, and then talking too much every lesson (a typical new teacher fail), I was losing my voice.

A voice is really the most important tool a teacher has. You sometimes hear about teachers who are vison impaired, teachers who are hearing impaired and about teachers who use wheelchairs. I've never heard about a teacher with a voice impairment. Teachers do really need a voice. As the weeks went on my own voice grew quieter (probably an improvement), hoarse and scratchy (ditto) and, most alarmingly, hurt when I spoke. I asked around in the staffroom, the font of all wisdom and gossip, and everyone cheerily had a tale of doom about a teacher they knew who had permanently damaged their voice and then never taught again.

Before the Easter break, I told the school's HR department about my voice problems and asked if there was any training they could recommend. I also politely requested if they could get move the leaf blowing sessions to after school or before school. In a true display of the hierarchy of a school (teachers are extremely low down on the food chain) I was firmly told that the groundskeepers' timetable, and use of leaf blower when a broom would be more efficient and quieter (but clearly not as much fun), was sacrosanct. I would have to suck it up. Unlike the gardeners and the leaves. I was also sent a brochure on voice health, which helpfully clarified that teachers who struggled most with voice issues were new teachers (yep) and middle-aged teachers (thanks).

To protect my voice, I developed that incredibly annoying teachers' habit of not asking for silence at the start of a lesson, but standing still, looking pained (as though I was struggling to control an enormous fart or dealing with an agonising period cramp), silently staring into the middle distance until the class simmered down. It worked a treat for everyone except Year 9s, who still needed a bellowing, or a beating, only one of which I was legally allowed to provide, until they were quiet.

9

THE BLOODY MEANING
OF THINGS

The new teacher always, and completely understandably, gets the worst classes in a school. There is no use throwing pearls before swine. The teachers who are proven high achievers are given the Year 12 classes which will get good results and add lustre to the school's academic reputation. They are also given the crucial year levels that take NAPLAN tests (Years 3, 5, 7 and 9) so that the school's rankings can be safeguarded or, even better, improved. Newbies get classes like my Year 11 English class, who cheerfully referred to themselves as being in the 'vegetable' English class. When I first heard this description I was shocked, but it was a term the kids used themselves. The Education Department and the school can spin the names of courses all they want, but kids can quickly spot if they are in the class with other kids who can't spell. I must clarify that neither I, the school or the other teachers ever used any derogatory term for such a class; the name was self-anointed and the more you objected to it, the more the kids used it. Kids in these classes are usually smart, but just not good at the arcane tasks required by schools. This actually works out fine for them, as only a minute percentage of the population write essays or do equations once they have left school. They even probably end up richer and happier because of it. UK celebrity TV host and columnist Jeremy Clarkson annually tweets when exam results come out that he got a C and two Es and now he's loaded and has the best job in the world. Sample size of one, so perfect proof. The students in these classes are generally lovely kids and it's here as a teacher you really can make a difference. The mini-Einsteins in the other classes would be fine even if you never turned up, but some of these students might actually learn something valuable from an interested teacher.

My Year 11 class (officially English 11.5) was happily made up of a some really personable, kind and smart students. It was 80 per cent boys. They were chatty, they were fun, and they really didn't want to be doing English. We spent lots of time discussing pop culture, only partly in the hope that I could find a 'text' to teach that would engage them. Eventually I chose a short, engaging, modern novel. Really short. Almost a novella. The only problem: no-one wanted to read the book.

Getting the kids to read out loud in class was torture for all of us, doing chapter quizzes about our individual reading was like pulling teeth, and supervising silent reading of the novel was noticeable for the fact that I never heard the rustle of a turning page. Finally, in desperation, I told them all to lie down the floor like they were back in primary school, and I would read the book out loud to them. We would have our very own story time. It took two weeks but they loved it and did actually pay attention. I cunningly stopped reading before the end of each lesson so we could discuss the literary aspects of the novel, and the author's use of techniques to engage the reader. However, I disguised these bits by posing question such as, 'Will your first love always let you down?', 'Mates over dates?' and that perennial dilemma of 'What makes you happy?' The big ideas by stealth. God, I loved teaching English.

It wasn't until the novel was done that we had to move onto the analysis part that always kills any enjoyment or appreciation of the book. Analysing a text is like explaining a joke. The animation and enjoyment drain out as you probe, and you are left with a lifeless corpse. In a horrible way, the more you study English literature, the less you want to read it. By the final year of my Arts degree (English major) I was incapable of reading any book unless it was wrapped in hot pink and used a puffy gold font on the cover. I couldn't read a literary prize nominee for years.

However, by teaching English I had signed up to suck the life out of books I enjoyed, and so I dutifully took the class through the literary deconstruction of the novel. 'That bloody meaning of things,' moaned one of my lovely students. 'It ruins everything.' As a reward, we watched the film adaptation of the novel. The film adaptation is the saviour of English teachers everywhere. As I fought with the DVD player to get the movie started, the class amused each other by fighting over who could recall the least of the plot.

Once, while I had been crouched in an undignified manner under my desk, trying to re-plug in the DVD player, wrestling with a tangle of black electrical cords, conscious that I was on my hand and knees, with my arse, not my best aspect, facing my class, I heard a phrase I dreaded.

'Do you know what I hate, Miss?' My mind boggled as I tried to wriggle out from under the desk backwards with some shred of dignity left. And without my knees cracking like gunfire. And without making the inadvertent groaning noises that sometimes escape me, like I am an old dog, when I undertake physical activity.

'What do you hate, Tom?' I replied, trying to sound pleasant and professional.

'Watching old people trying and failing to use technology.'

I had no answer and couldn't even use my hard stare. I hoped that my rear poker face had been up to the job.

As I wriggled out from under the desk this time, amid the usual cries of 'we weren't up to this bit yet,' I tried to shush the class and find the right spot in the film. As a married woman I normally never get to use the television remote control. In fact, I haven't been in command of it for years. Watching films in class proved that my technology skills had not kept pace even with the school's antiquated DVD player. Students had become used to shouting out instructions such as: 'Choose select scene, now fast forward, not so much. Stop, stop, stop!'

'Can we do *American Psycho* next?' they asked hopefully.

'The film that's R rated, that you are too young to see?' I confirmed, primly. 'No.'

'But we've all already seen it,' they said.

'It's still a no.'

My English class was such a generous, open-hearted and fun group of students. It genuinely was a privilege to spend so much time with them every day and hear about their lives. As a teacher, you are in that sweet spot of being an interested adult but not too interested or too invested. While my own children never want to tell me anything, students are often willing to share a surprising amount about their life with their teachers. Sometimes even information that was tangentially relevant to their education.

They also told me exactly what they wanted to do in the summer, and then with their lives. I heard a lot about their weekends and their parties and often, like a lawyer, I had to ask them to stop talking as it would harm their defence if I knew too much.

One of the real privileges of teaching is the opportunity to be engaged and involved in the lives of your students. It's also a way in which you, as the teacher, can be a force for good. Again, it's not in a showy way that might be the subject of inspiring novel or screenplay. I don't think I have ever boosted a child's ATAR so dramatically that a new career opened up and that student became a researcher who cured a type of cancer. (If I did, however, please get in touch with me via my publishers and we will work on that screenplay together.) Instead, your engagement and interest can make the student feel better about themselves, can give them the warm glow and spark of self-belief to know that an adult (who is not related to them) is concerned and cares about them. It's obviously the wafting rose petal of soft skills and can't be quantified or coded. It probably can't even be taught. Fortunately, though, most teachers have it and deploy their engagement and interest daily, nurturing the students in their care. It's not very dramatic, but I think the best way I managed to help my students as a teacher was by being interested and invested in them. Forging connections with my Year 11 class improved my life, and I think it improved theirs too.

It was also rewarding to unpack how to write a clear sentence and how an author could manipulate the reader through language choices. The insights of my students were often arresting, and class discussion had fluency and emotion. Even if their written responses were unable to replicate these moments, the thinking, if not the work submitted for marking, showed learning. I felt upset that even within the generous scope of the curriculum, I could not properly capture and quantify this achievement. Instead, I tried to take comfort in the fact that the happy memories of English lessons for these students might be one of the many unquantifiable outcomes of education.

Later, after I had learnt much more from my students, I was deemed to have been adequately blooded as a teacher and was trusted with a class that was academically skilled at English, as well as proven to get good results in English assessments. We were studying *Pride and Prejudice* (and not only, but partly, so I could later watch Colin Firth in his damp white shirt, sideburns and his lust-worthy stately home). After a slow start, which I enlivened with a few lowbrow 'Which Bennet sister are you?' quizzes, we moved onto characterisation.

We were examining Mrs Bennet, a prototype embarrassing mother. 'My mother is exactly like Mrs Bennet,' said one girl, and then spent an enlightening ten minutes explaining why. I couldn't wait for parent–teacher interviews that term.

One of the main joys of teaching is the camaraderie of the teacher's staffroom. In the first semester I was allocated a space in the 'general' staffroom, where I sat near maths teachers, science teachers and a French teacher. Their desks were tidy and they looked on disapprovingly as my pile of untouched marking, including a poster project I had misguidedly set my Year 7 class, overwhelmed my desk and spilled onto the floor, attempting to colonise their desks. They were kind (one lovely maths teacher agreed to sit in and supervise one of my lessons during her free period so that I could nip out and see my child for thirty minutes during a school performance) and they had good tips about how to navigate the school. But they weren't exactly kindred spirits.

They didn't enjoy my shaggy dog tales and they didn't sympathise at all with my co-curricular woes. At a private school, teachers are made to supervise or run a co-curricular activity. A co-curricular sounds fancy; it's the kind of thing you hear students talking about putting on their 'application for college'. It means all the school activities that aren't classes in the curriculum. I don't know why it is 'co' curricular rather than an 'extra' curricular, but I'm figuring that if I've never bothered to look it up before now then no-one reading this will care either. Co-curriculars cover bands, choirs, orchestras, musical productions, drama productions, sports, debating, mooting and I suppose an unlimited number of activities depending upon the needs of the students and their parents. If you are at a school where skiing, sailing and equestrian activities are part of the co-curriculars then some of the parents must be minted. Most schools have their own quirky co-curricular, so it will be up to you as to how unstartled you want to look when you find out the students all play bagpipes, do rifle practice or yodel.

Usually, every teacher theoretically must do one co-curricular, but there are co-curriculars and co-curriculars. There is also always that one teacher who must be sleeping with all of the Council of Governors and has a laughably ridiculous easy co-curricular, like taking a Year 12 class for gelati on hot days. To create the illusion of choice for the teaching staff, I had been asked to nominate the co-curricular I wanted to do. The answer 'None – I want to be able to watch my own children participate in their co-curriculars', was not an option on the form. As an ex-civil litigation lawyer, I put down mooting and then debating. For my third choice I wrote, 'I am terrible at sport and hate it, so anything without a ball.' That was true. I have two left feet, no hand–eye coordination and loathe team sport. My idea of exercise is reading a hardback novel in bed. When working in an office and subjected to mandatory chat about the footy tipping every Monday morning, I volunteered to get the coffees so I could skip the football chat completely.

Naturally, I was assigned to softball. Two terms of it (Term 1 and Term 4), with two training sessions a week after school, a fun hour every week drawing up the team list and sending emails about the weekly match details, following up with emails from parents and students about why they weren't in the team, or, if they were in the team, about why they couldn't play that week, plus Saturday morning matches that, on some simply demonic weekends, started at 7.30am at a far-flung school and finished at midday. I had somehow not envisioned that working as a teacher would mean hiring a babysitter to come on Saturday mornings to look after my own children, so that I could supervise other people's children playing school sport.

The weeknight trainings were bad enough (the balls, the whistles, the heartiness, plus the jangling keys for locking up the sports kit in the correct sheds) but the Saturday matches were a new level of torment. Firstly, there was the small talk (and sports small talk at that) with the parents. Then there was the continued fear that I might have to use my first aid kit. When I had proudly attended my first day-long St John's Ambulance first aid course (a compulsory part of teacher registration because, you know, teachers have to be able to do everything and fix anything), I had come home and boastfully told my medical husband about my new-found skills. He questioned me about what I had been told to do in various circumstances and listened attentively.

'Georgie,' he said kindly and crushingly. 'Please just keep your mobile phone in your pocket. That way, you can call an ambulance straight away if anything happens.'

After that confidence booster, I was always anxious that I would have to actually put my non-existent first aid skills to use, and I spent the first few trainings anxiously searching though my kit, trying to identify everything while I was still calm, in control and there was no blood spurting. Softball finally became manageable when I reluctantly engaged in parental small talk and found out that one keen mother really seemed to know the rules. When questioned, she shyly admitted to being an ex-nationals player. I handed over the clipboard and retreated happily to the corner while she expertly managed the team.

Term 2, when softball mercifully went into abeyance, was much smoother, helped by all the free time I had now that I wasn't locking the softball kit up in the sheds. My life was a bit like the gag about making existence in your tiny apartment better by moving in a cow, then a pig and finally a horse, and then moving them all out so you could revel in the silence and the space. I knew where all staff toilets were, and I'd found out how to use the staff photocopiers and the online excursion forms, achievements that probably warranted a ticker tape parade. Term 2 is also normally mercifully shorter than Term 1, and you can coast for a bit on some of your earlier preparation at the start of the year.

Even so, as Term 2 raced past, I was enormously surprised to have survived the first semester and had almost got to grips with the names of all 125 of my students. I had become desensitised to the endless marking and the feeling of never being on top of the workload. I even accepted that Sundays were marking days, and that television was a treat for other people (like my Year 11 class). My classes knew me, and we had that kind of relationship where I just had to threateningly wave the grammar textbook at the Year 8 class during silent reading in order to keep them quiet. The shorthand of a good relationship. Timetables often change mid-year, and my school was no exception. I kept most of my classes but was delighted to find my staffroom allocation had changed from a general one to one exclusively filled with teachers from the humanities faculty.

My kind of people. People with glasses, who liked talking about books and who had a healthy, cynical disregard for authority and motivational slogans. People who liked wordplay, puns and reading inadvertently amusing errors out loud from their marking for their neighbours to enjoy. People who positively adored finding malapropisms. People who the rest of the staff probably found intolerable, and so we were all locked up together.

Teaching is a strange job where you work in isolation from your peers. You never really see anyone else teach, weave that magical inspiration with a class. A bit like the light in the refrigerator syndrome, if you can see it happening, then its's not truly happening properly. As a learner teacher you do get the opportunity to watch other teachers in action, but your presence in the classroom means that the class is a little self-conscious, and the lesson isn't really natural.

We did once discuss having the head of faculty spending one lesson each term observing us in our classrooms to see how we taught. Embarrassingly, he said that he didn't need to make a time to observe my class, as he could always hear exactly what was going on in it from his own classroom. The rest of the English faculty laughed, in the quite supportive manner of English teachers, and then everyone embarked on an animated discussion about whether it was my voice, my laugh or the chatter from my class that was most penetrating sound through their classroom walls.

Usually, others can't really hear what is happening in another classroom. There are, however, some school sounds that spread down the hallways and waft out into the playground. There is the special sycophantic titter when a teacher makes a bad joke. You can hear the scraping of chairs as the teacher gets the class to arrange their chairs in a circle, and you can hear the occasional student telling off, where a teacher hisses at the miscreant in the hallway as the rest of that class falls eerily quiet trying to overhear the details. But otherwise, unless you arrive in a classroom and see some great notes written on the whiteboard, you don't really know how the others are doing it. Other people's classrooms are as mysterious as other people's marriages.

Especially as a new teacher you need to debrief, to ask questions, borrow task sheets and bitch, and the staffroom is where it all takes place. Our staffroom leader had the unruffled Zen air of knowing the content, knowing how to best teach it and knowing how to connect with students. His was the voice of experience, and every recess and lunch that I didn't have yard duty, I would interrupt his marking to ask questions.

'Is it unfair to grant an extension to a student who has no reason for not doing the work?'

No, was the answer because those students will never spend the whole extension diligently doing the work. They will throw it together at the last minute anyway.

'Who gets the A plus? How can I justify it to the student who wants but can't get an A?'

Give the A plus to the ones with the spark. Keep a de-identified A plus from a different year group and show it to the resentful student. Ask them if they can honestly tell the difference between their work and the example. If they can, they might deserve an A plus, if they can explain why the other work is better. If they can't, tell them they don't.

'What to do with the over-anxious parent?'

Drown them with work. Give them their own reading list and pile it on. Keep them busy and silent.

'How do I react when it's obvious the kid's mother has written the essay?'

Don't write down that accusation. Get the kid to stay back after class and you can ask them to go home to tell their mum that the essay got a C, but you will accept a resubmitted essay. If you get a substitute essay that is worse than the first, you can give the replacement one a B with some encouraging comments written on the side.

The staffroom was a safe space. Students were not allowed, and our immediate boss, the faculty head, was safely isolated in his own office cave. While you do miss a class when they move on at the end of the year, the teachers in the staffroom are your real constant companions. The grief when they move to another school is real, and is the reason why most teachers, when they find a congenial, collegial atmosphere (and a contract), stay put in their school. In the staffroom, teachers plotted their own dreams, their ideal classes, and tried to maintain their vision of teaching excellence while being swept along on the currents of the term.

While being trained as a teacher and as part of mandatory

annual professional learning, we were always exhorted to 'reflect' on our teaching, which meant thinking about what had gone well and what had gone wrong, and how we could improve it next time (if there was a next time). It was good advice and obviously had the potential to create better teaching. It was hard to find the time to do this properly, and also challenging to differentiate and understand the difference between teaching that had improved student outcomes, and teaching that the students had enjoyed. Sometimes a class would be engaged with a unit of work but it wouldn't be reflected in better results or understanding in their summative tasks, which in case you are not currently in a classroom, means the kind of test or assignment that goes towards your grade.

In judging how effective your teaching has been, there are many variables, one of which is the problem of recognising the human (or student) factor at play. A student who arrives in your English class showing tendencies towards dyslexia is probably going to leave your English class still struggling to spell. You might help them to commit some key words to memory, and give them some tips to help, but you won't be able to fix the problem. In assessing the effectiveness of your teaching it's tempting to blame everything on a 'bad class' but it's then salutary when you see that class excel for another teacher and realise it really was just something about you and your teaching that didn't quite work.

I have been fortunate enough to teach classes with smart, talented and insightful students, who wrote clearly and persuasively. While some of those wonderful students may have gained something from being taught by me, in all honesty I think they had the talent already, and I just really held the gate open and stayed out of the way, shouting encouragement as they raced through to the finish line. I think, upon reflection, the students which I have had the most impact on have been those who were struggling. Those who hadn't been blessed at birth by a fairy godmother with the gift of having schoolwork come easily to them.

Often these 'strugglers' are more challenging students, as by the time they reach secondary school, they already think that they are no good academically and have developed some defensive avoidance strategies. Understandably, they often put up a protective barrier of disinterest and the appearance of not trying. It's a camouflage that I am very familiar with, as it is one that I often drape myself in.

It was these struggling students that brought out my most evangelical feelings about being an English teacher. While I have waxed lyrical about inspiring my students to read for pleasure, and the power of literature to improve every aspect of life, I doubt that I have truly changed the destiny of any of my students through this preaching. Where I think I have made a practical improvement to some students has been via the more prosaic skill of writing. I can say proudly that some of my students can now, after spending time in my classroom, express themselves clearly using the written word. They can write sentences that can be understood. They can persuade people with their words. They can write a caption on an Instagram post that really engages. They can compose a concise email to a future employer.

When I started teaching English, I thought that I would be the most help to students by instructing them about literary analysis. Or by showing them how to construct a powerfully persuasive essay, replete with supportive quotations from the text. These are the skills needed by university undergraduates and, eventually, for a select unfortunate few, by academia. However, this sort of writing is esoteric and arcane. Essay writing has hallowed conventions, and writing a good essay is a technical skill that will only serve you well when you need to write an essay. Spoiler alert, most adults don't write essays. Constructing an essay is a bit like doing a triple jump, a strange skill set nurtured predominantly at senior school and nowhere else.

It took some teaching time before I realised that while most students had been taught to compose sentences when they were in primary school, having the capital letter and the full stop down pat, they did not know what to put in their sentence. It's not until you spend night after night reading tortured prose that you truly appreciate how fiendishly difficult the English language can be to operate. There is so much freedom, and an intoxicating absence of rules. And, like many things in life, having too much choice can make the decision about what to put in and what to leave out really challenging.

I hope that students in my English classes have learnt how to say what they mean. I would talk with them, chat with them and write encouraging and constructive criticism all over their written work. They learnt that short sentences are the best. Short sentences are clear. Short sentences rule.

They say what you mean. They are hard to get tangled in. They let you make a point. For variation, once you have made a point, you can write a longer sentence with a subclause. You still aim always to make your point, but then, once it is made, you can introduce the idea of shades of grey, of the uncertainty and the factors which, on the other hand, might expand your initial point. They also learn that clear writing does not involve the use of every vocabulary building word they know. Short simple words are easy to understand. Short words are the best. Superlatives can suffocate meaning, and enthusiastically sprinkling a sentence with polysyllabic words does not make the writer seem smarter. It can make the writer look uncertain, as if they are hiding behind their words, or it can simply make the writer look as though they have spent too long playing with the thesaurus function of their computer and too little thinking about what they have to say. It was often the students who were most uncertain of their skills who composed impenetrable, defensive sentences. Coaxing and encouraging them could, often, in one semester, produce students who could write what they meant.

Part of the joy and satisfaction in teaching English is that you get to instruct students on things that might be really useful to them- wherever life takes them. It's teachers to the rescue - offering instruction on things that will make life better for all. Some of these include:

• Knowing how to deliver a speech. (This is still an option in many of the senior Australian curriculums but if I was King of the World, I'd make it mandatory.) Everyone will have the chance to deliver one speech in their life – even if it's a farewell speech in the work canteen or a eulogy.

• Know when to use an apostrophe. And, most crucially (especially in case kids ever end up chalking up grocery signs) at least know and be able to apply the phrase 'when in doubt, leave it out'.

• Know how to spell their own frequently misspelt words. Or, at least, recognise the need to look those words up when it's important. Based on my current fervent reading of social media, I suggest many add the word 'divine' (it is not spelt 'devine') to their list.

• Know where their local library is and be prepared to fight like a banshee to keep it well funded.

• Know the difference between formal and informal language, and appreciate where to use each type.

This sort of teaching was actually the most rewarding of all. It can take almost a lifetime to realise that most people will never have an original literary insight about a text, and also that it really doesn't matter. That insightful analysis wasn't going to change the world anyway. Most people also can't write clearly, but they can be taught to do so. Clear writing can not only change their own life for the better, but it might also change the world. It took me a while to realise that these slow, incremental and basic lessons are the true rewards of teaching. It would be astounding to have a Hollywood-style moment of revelation, where a struggling student makes an amazing breakthrough, and fame and fortune followed. But that never happened to me, and I don't think that it happens to most teachers. Instead, there's slow progress, where after weeks and weeks a student can do one simple task better because you were in the room teaching them, encouraging them and helping them to get there. That small thing will be used for the rest of the student's life, and will help them to achieve their dreams and realise their potential. It's not fireworks, but rather gently switching on a rather dull-looking lamp in the corner. It's hard to see the reward straight away, but years later when you read a business Instagram post by a former student that concisely explains their message in ten short words, you can feel a warm glow of achievement. The rewards are seldom spectacular in teaching, but teachers know that already, because, as their coffee mugs say, they aren't in it for the money or the status, they are in it for the students.

This is not
a prop.
It is for the
drama teacher's
coffee.

10

I'M NOT THAT SICK

In normal office jobs, when you are sick you phone your boss (making sure you sound sick, giving up some fruity coughs to ram the point home), and then you send a follow-up email to the HR department. If you had an amazingly busy day, with meetings with very important people, you would also email those people to explain that sadly you won't be in and will reschedule the meetings for a later date. If you are a bit important, or someone on your team likes you, your meetings can even be taken for you. Normal office jobs are lovely. You will need to catch up on what you missed later, but that's generally not too onerous.

I am aware, having a medical husband and having been a stay-at-home mother, that not all jobs are like that. Sometimes, you've just got to soldier on. Sometimes you're not allowed to be sick; you need to produce a positive Covid test; your supervisor will shout at you; you don't get sick leave. But occasionally, even if you are a Very Important Person, you can just collapse and others will have to pick up the slack (or you let your toddlers watch ABC Kids continuously and eat Chicken Crimpy biscuits all day).

Teaching falls into a special category of shit jobs where calling in sick will cause you more work than just going in to work. Teachers have to be really, really unwell before they want to take the day off. This is because only you know what each of your classes are doing, or what they should to be doing. You need to prepare a written instruction sheet for each class about the lesson plan, complete with links to the resources that will be needed. You will probably have at least six classes that day, so that is six lessons to prepare when your throat feels like you have swallowed razor blades and you can't think.

If you are an English teacher and your instruction is for 'class to continue with their individual reading', you can be sure that over half the class will not remember to bring their books, and the relief-teacher will kill you when they next see you. Relief lessons are usually taken by your fellow teachers in their valuable one free lesson a day. By not turning up you have already wrecked their day and ruined their chance of getting on top of their immediate marking and planning priorities. They hate you already, so don't make it worse for them by providing a poorly prepared instruction sheet. Hiring a professional temporary relief-teacher to cover the lesson is expensive for schools and only happens if there is a flu pandemic, stress crisis or whole group of teachers is scheduled time away for training, marking or camp.

Tips for the ideal relief lesson to be set for any class are set out below, based on my experience about relief lessons that I loved, but mainly (of course) about relief lessons I had to take for other teachers that really got on my tits.

A relief lesson should be able to be conducted silently by the class and not require any special assistance from the teacher.

No-one ever knows in advance who the lesson will be assigned to, and odds on it will be given to someone who isn't an expert in the field. Not every teacher will have a lovely experience like mine, when I was given a maths class where I was unable to provide any assistance. To be fair, any maths class above Year 6 level would be beyond my help. I asked the class who was the best at maths. The class always knows, and is always pretty fair, so I gave that student the whiteboard marker (there is no greater symbol of trust) and my desk, while I sat at that student's desk and enjoyed the expert lesson she provided to the class. In retrospect I should have sent that girl my pay for the day, but it was probably a valuable learning experience for her, and that is priceless, surely.

It is guaranteed that the poor teacher who has been shoehorned into taking your relief lesson had big, big plans for their forty-five minutes of freedom. They might have done a wee, or even had a cup of coffee. They might have needed to do some photocopying for Year 8 or sorted out their lesson planning for the Year 11 double later that afternoon. They might have needed to finalise the excursion consent forms or book the IT suite for a lesson tomorrow.

They could have had to call a parent. They might have even wanted to start doing some marking, even though it's not enough time to have a proper go at the pile. They do not need to be teaching your content. Some teachers set a 'watch this clip' lesson and think they are doing you a favour, but a rolling screen is not the hypnotic panacea it once was for children who already have hours of screen time a day on their phones. They now have a high tolerance for crap on TikTok but a low tolerance for documentaries. Sitting at the back of a darkened room saying shush to a class while watching bad actors in wigs pretending to be explorers is not conducive to anything except irritation.

A relief lesson should not require any external resources. If the school has an email system, take a photo of the exact work you want done, and the extra pages, links or resources needed and email it through.

If you have asked the students to use any external resources at all, even their textbook, half of them will have 'forgotten' it and have to take a long and noisy trip to their lockers to get the book. If you require the class to complete watching a film, set a back-up activity as tech-gremlins will surely ruin the whole planned film experience. If you are a drama teacher and you set a task involving your students wearing costumes, then don't bother coming to school tomorrow, as the relieving teacher who has had to supervise the folding and return of the costumes will kill you when they next see you. And not just with that prop knife.

A relief lesson should be something the students understand and are immersed in already.

It can't hurt to spell this out in the instructions to the relieving teacher. It is some unwritten student law (like never go to the toilet in a break, always go just when the teacher starts explaining a crucial concept) that students in a relief class always deny they know what is going on or that they have done any work at all on that area. For example, if the relief-teacher is instructed that the students have been covering Australian Federation all term and are to write some summary notes in the lesson for an upcoming test, and they are foolish enough to say in front of the class: 'I gather you have been studying Federation,' as one the class will deny it. 'What's the Federation?' they will ask. I'm not sure whether the motivation is forgetfulness, wishful thinking or just an honest desire to have some fun at the expense of the relief-teacher. Never, ever get drawn into a discussion about it with the class, even if you are staring right at their posters about the Fathers of Federation (some seriously beardy dudes, like ZZ Top in suits) which are all over the classroom walls. Just say, 'Well, you have lots of fun stuff to learn then!' in an upbeat voice, showing that you are a take-no-prisoners kind of bitch, and therefore ideally suited to being a relief-teacher.

Don't let the class grumble on about their usual teacher either, as it's unprofessional and bad for school morale, plus you wouldn't want another teacher to allow the class to grumble on about you. But ... if you hear a real gem in the first second of whining before you shut it down, then that's your bonus for the day, and hey, you can't unhear it.

A relief lesson should not be for a Health and PE class.

For Health and PE classes the relieving teacher is not a yummy mummy and so does not have the advantage of being in their Lululemons and sneakers already. They, the poor things, will be in professional clothes and then will have to supervise the horror of the changing rooms, whistles, balls, plus whatever terrible activity is going on while in their normal restrictive teaching clothes. If it's a health lesson in a classroom or gym then they are probably going to have to teach some form of sex ed to an unknown class. Although English teachers generally have nerves of steel for such stuff because of all the intricate details we always have to explain (every year the concept of maidenheads seems to always come up, and literature is absolutely oozing with sex), and the science teachers are obviously hardened to expounding on the anatomical details as well, there are plenty of staff who did not go into teaching to talk about these issues with random teenagers. Spare them. Just come in. You don't have much marking to do at home so you can rest after school. I'd say that to your faces, but I'm too slow, too weak, too fat, too unfit and too scared. Plus, I'm a fair way into the book now, so I think I'm probably safe.

A relief lesson should mention that you have emailed the

senior students about the change as well.

At any school where the students have laptops or iPads and their own school emails and electronic management systems, teachers already know that they are in frequent and helpful contact with their students (i.e. they are the electronic slaves of the students). The Year 11 and 12s will email you in a panic if you aren't there, so it's easier to head this off at the pass with a reassuring email explaining you will be away, this is what you will be asking them to do, and no, you haven't finished their marking yet. If any of your students email you back with a 'get well soon' you can earmark that kid for greatness and a favourable expression of your discretion in the future.

11

I'M SO PLEASED WE
COULD MEET

My new staffroom friends were full of advice about how to prepare for my first round of parent–teacher interviews. Their tips were essential, but like so many aspects of teaching, I had to learn from just from doing.

After seven years of teaching, I am now a small, short war veteran of parent–teacher interviews. They are another essential teacher skill and extra stress of the job that is hard to properly understand when you decided to teach. You need to spend several nights before preparing, collating all the data about each student. The interviews are also always after school, so you teach a full day and then stay on at work until 9.30pm for several nights. If teaching at a private school, you will be expected to wear a suit (or, if you are a maths teacher, your smartest cardigan). A dirty secret of the private school system is that the whopping school fees are not reflected in the teacher salaries. In fact, pay is often lower in the private system. Despite this, private schools like their teachers to be dressed as the professionals they aren't paid as, and especially so on parent–teacher interview nights, when teachers are on display and are part of the shiny extras that the parents are shelling out for.

Sometimes, if you are lucky, there will be food laid on for dinner in the staffroom, and if parents do not run late or have too many questions, you will get to bolt down a meal halfway through the night and then anxiously fret that you are breathing onion fumes over everyone for the rest of the evening. Usually, your voice gives out after the first night of parent–teacher interviews due to all the talking required. After you have seen several parents, your patter gets smoother and you can repeat the opening phrase 'they are a lovely class, I have so enjoyed teaching them, and we have just finished our unit on the novel', which can give you a slightly trippy déjà vu feeling as you suddenly stop roaming the sunlight prairie in your mind, your yellow gingham dress blowing in the wind, and wonder if you have said that phrase already to the current parents, or whether there is indeed a crack in the space–time continuum.

You can usually access the list of bookings in advance so you know the names of the parents attending at each time slot. It is a good idea to take along a class list for each class with a headshot of the students, because if you are teaching a full load (six subjects) with full classes (meant to be capped at twenty-five but sometimes up to thirty) you will have around 125 students to mentally keep track of. More than once, without the class list at hand, I have struggled to remember exactly who the student was. One particularly bad year I had three blonde girls called Sophie in one class, who all sported matching ponytails and chirpy dispositions. Once your opening patter is sorted, you can spend the first minute of the interview scrutinising the parents and trying to work out who the student most resembles. My other tip is, regardless of how old the parent looks, never, never, never assume they are the grandparent. Even if they look like Methuselah and arrive wearing their Boer War service medals, always talk about their child, rather than their grandchild.

Even if there are two adults perched opposite you on the interview table, also don't presume that all the interested adults are present. If you have the child's father and his girlfriend present and get started with the chitchat, the child's mother will be justifiably furious when she arrives (and also when she has to drag another chair in from the edge of the room to sit on). Some schools encourage the children to come to the interview too. Unless they are needed to act as a translator for their parents, I think that this is a bad idea. You already have had many interactions with the student and opportunities to talk to them privately after class or during lunch, so they already know what you think about their work. Parent–teacher interviews are for you to frankly and openly discuss the work done by a student with their parents, and to offer constructive advice and feedback. Having the child in question present obviously inhibits this frank discussion. It's what I imagine it would be like to have your child present during marriage counselling.

Parent–teacher interviews are best when there is a bell to mark the end of each session so there is a clear signal for the time-hoggers to move on. Otherwise, some parents will settle in with hours of anxious questions about their little darling and refuse to give anyone else a turn. Your whole evening will then run behind time and you will irritate all of the other parents, whose planned interviews will receive less time.

Interviews also provide a fun opportunity to see exactly why students are the way they are and allow you to practise your empathy skills. Invariably, the parents of the students who are perpetually late and disorganised arrive at their interview at the wrong time, or after their scheduled time has nearly finished.

A further challenge of teaching English is that a parent may accuse you, someone who has had the little darling in their class for a mere sixteen weeks, of being solely responsible for their child's inability to spell, organise a coherent sentence, write essays or read the works of the classical Western canon in bed at night. Reassurances that you are 'working on that' with the student tend to be brushed off. After several years of parent– teacher interviews I finally twigged that attack is the best form of defence, and I used to sanctimoniously declare that the latest research proved that English skills were linked to early exposure to reading. Toddlers who have stories read to them every night and grow up in a house full of books with parents who read for pleasure do better in literacy scores. It's so hard, I would sigh, wistfully, looking deep into the guilty parental eyes, to overcome a lack of early literacy immersion.

The other type of parent–teacher interview I did, and

which became more frequent as the years went on, were the happy ones. By then I was calmer, and if I couldn't recall the precise details of an assignment I felt braver and was able to admit that and move on. One of my fellow teachers used to declare that 'on some interview nights we need wine and cheese' and she was right. Sometimes, the night were more like a social occasion, and you felt a camaraderie with the parents. We were all on the same page, we all liked their child and we all joked knowingly about the 'lost essay'. Parenthood is a rough gig and except for an annual commercialised day of homemade cards and breakfast in bed, there is often not much feedback or gratitude. Acknowledgement of a job well done from a teacher at an interview night can sometimes be the only warm glow of achievement that a parent gets all year. Parent–teacher interviews provide an opportunity for another adult who knows your child to tell you that it's going to be okay, and that is a moment to be celebrated. Sometimes too, the parents will tell you that their child likes being taught by you, and that's another warm feeling you can hug to your chest when you next have to stay up late marking on a Sunday night.

12

BRING OUT THE DISCO WHISTLE

As if marking and lesson planning isn't enough fun to be had out of hours, occasionally the year group you supervise will be attending a school disco, social, prom or formal. You will, of course, as your devotion to teaching covers all hours of the day and night (and your desire for a permanent contract and the ability to pay off your mortgage know no bounds), ask the Vice Principal if you could help out.

The school will be so desperate to get enough staff to supervise that you are likely to be roped in anyway, so you might as well volunteer before being conscripted and earn some Brownie points. There will be a meeting about things you need to do on the night, and then an unofficial chat about things you *really* need to do. But, if you were a teenager once, you probably know what those things are anyway.

Not least as before the event, the students are all given a

list of firm rules, and then the school, and the teachers in turn, try their hardest to enforce those rules. Some conventions and expectations have changed over time, and I don't even think the Catholic sector require students to slow dance a ruler's length apart (to leave some room for the Holy Spirit) anymore.

If you teach design, art or are just unlucky, you may have to help students decorate the hall or gym for the big night. This will be hell with duct tape and a staple gun. There will always be one control freak female teacher and a clique of bossy female students who have an overly grand decorating scheme that they have been planning on Pinterest for weeks. 'We'll duct tape up the windows, flood the gym and release some fluorescent fish to really catch the light.' These bitches will never do all the cleaning up afterwards, so just say no. Kids will have the same socially awkward time with the school's old glitter ball and the foil stars that are already in the art department cupboard from last year. Even if the place is done up like a Kardashian wedding, it will still be a school event filled with school students. As it should be.

At many schools, an organising committee will be formed. This will provide students with the valuable life experience of what social organising committees are like in the real world, so they can know never to voluntarily sign up to one again. The committee will be dominated by the popular kids who will come up with outlandish ideas that have other, less popular students being driven to Spotlight and Big W at 9pm by their doting parents before they (the less popular kids and the more doting parents) spend all weekend making pompoms in the theme colours for the big event.

The advertising posters and the tickets will have to be pre-vetted by the school to avoid references to drugs, booze and inappropriate role models. Sometimes an unlucky teacher is also made to trawl through the proposed playlist of songs looking for questionable references to sex and drugs, an almost impossible and thankless task.

No work will be done by any student in the week leading up to the big event. If it is a wing-ding for Year 11 and 12 students, the female student body will spend the week prior to the event beautifying their student body. Spray tans will be mandatory, and the luckiest teachers will work in classrooms with windows that open so they can get some fresh air to dilute the pungent rotting flesh stink of fake tan. The saddest moments are when bad tan jobs happen to good girls, who turn up in your lesson looking upset and a brilliant-orange colour, and you plead with the rest of the class to stop singing the Oompa Loompa songs from *Charlie and the Chocolate Factory*.

Fake fingernails are also required and brilliantly shellacked nails are furtively hidden from view, as clearly it would be impossible to attend a dance in a new dress without a matching mani. Fake eyelashes will be applied in the days leading up to the event, lending some lessons an Arabian Nights air, as so many of the girls look like camels with their three-centimetre-long lashes. There is no point in asking if anyone is wearing fake lashes in contravention of the school rules, as the host of the new centipede-like lashes will struggle to open their eyelids, peer at you through their forest of mink, and deny your suggestion in a hurt tone, as unnatural as their look. Serious on fleek brows also multiply, and for once you can teach feeling that people are intently listening as, if their perky, raised eyebrows are anything to go on, they are all very interested indeed.

Many female students get their makeup professionally applied and their hair styled by a hairdresser, adding hundreds of dollars to the cost of the night, as well as adding immeasurably to the anticipation which cannot possibly be met by the function.

At many schools, formals also require the purchase of frocks at a rate and volume that suggests a reality TV wedding show, rather than a function for teenagers. Female students will insist on the purchase of a dress, shoes, handbag and jewellery for the formal, and then another dress (and shoes, etc) for the after party. Even though I'm sure many teenagers plead with their parents that 'the outfit is an investment, I will wear it so many times in the next few years', everyone really knows that is a lie. The cost per wear will never work out to be reasonable, but the magical belief that this outfit really is the one time when it will happen is another example of hope triumphing over experience.

By contrast, I only had one dress for my wedding day (and bought a pair of shoes that I covered in a matching white fabric which made them too small, so my saintly and much put-upon brother wore them with his footy socks at night while watching telly to break them in for me). The first time I heard the 'after party dress' story I told a pair of female students that I felt sorry for their parents.

'You oldies all stick together,' was the unsurprising and

well-deserved riposte. It's a charge I couldn't deny. I *am* old, and empathise with the parents, rather than the students. Attending a party at 2am and, in all honesty, doing anything at all after 11pm, fills me with horror.

My own formal was different: lots of girls sewed their own dresses, many of them genuine 1980s horrors, with black velvet sweetheart bodices above a tartan silk puffy skirt. Girls who were unbelievably well off had their silk purchased in Thailand by a globe-trotting relative. You put on your own makeup, either alone or in a giggling group with friends, and then scrunched and swirled your permed fringe before blasting the whole do with hairspray. We looked like the 1980s schoolgirls we were (and imagined that we looked like we were teenagers in a John Hughes film).

Girls today favour sleek and revealing evening gowns, couple with impeccable hair, makeup and spray tans, so at their formals they more closely resemble contestants in the evening gown section of Miss Universe. Much like modern weddings, the photos also appear to have become the primary reason for the formal. In fact, there is probably no need for the actual formal; you could just get all dressed up and have the the photos (taken by doting parents before at home and then at the before party, and by the professional photographers at the event, and taken by everyone at the function ceaselessly the whole night) without actually bothering to hold an actual formal at all.

If it's a Year 7, 8 or 9 event, preparations are calmer. Every student debuts a new hairstyle and a drenching of perfume or aftershave. Serious amounts of makeup are applied, which again means that you have to try really hard to recognise your own students. A scent of excitement and Lynx will fill the hall. Some of the boys will spend hours wrestling and playfighting, while their female peers stand in small groups and chat. Many students will have adopted the latest body-baring fashion (crop tops, cut outs, plunging cleavage, truly short shorts). Just look the kids in their eyes only. You will, as if your teacher's badge and cardigan didn't give you already, know that you are really old and from another generation as you cluck disapprovingly with your fellow teachers out of earshot about 'what young people are wearing today' and 'what kind of parents would let their children go out of the house looking like this'. As you do this of course, you have to block out memories of the outfits you know your own children wear.

The teachers may not be given actual rulers anymore for discipline, but they do discreetly smell breath and monitor behaviour for signs of boozing, and punch bowls have gone out of fashion at most sensible schools. (Which is a bit sad as 'someone spiked the punch' must be one the classic excuses of all time.) Like all aspects of teaching, there is a limit to what you can actually do to modify the behaviour of teenagers, and what the parents of those students actually enable you to do. If students have been given two drinks by their parents before they arrive, despite the strongly worded letter from the principal sent out before the event, there is little you can do about alcohol that is already in the student's bloodstream. You can, of course, do something about drink and drugs that have not yet been ingested. The rise of the camera on the smart phone has done much to assist here (a good news story for once) as most kids today are wary of a photo of them vomiting out of control being broadcast across all social media channels. Arriving to investigate potential bad behaviour with a phone in hand also presents an air of menace and evidence gathering that tends to quell the masses.

Hopefully, the students get loaded after the event or not at all, and you can spend the night the way teachers are expected to: looking and feeling dowdy, truthfully saying 'I hardly recognised you,' to overly made-up students and dancing like the dag you are on the edge of the dancefloor, a suitable distance from the kids. You can also patrol the loos and the gardens outside, a job that you get to practise during the daylight hours at least once a week when you are on yard duty.

I was completely keyed-up with anxiety before my first school social supervision, anxious about how I would maintain discipline and stop the pashing, the drinking and the rest. However, the biggest crisis of the night turned out to be some of the small props from the photo booth going missing. The biggest hardship was staying back late to pull up all of the duct-taped electric cables and decorations so that the hall could be used again tomorrow morning. It was a real reminder that although everyone often thinks the worst of teenagers, most of them don't deserve their bad press. They are, on the whole, empathetic, kind kids, who stopped to talk to me when I awkwardly walked past them, alone, old and badly dressed.

Don't make
me use
my teacher
voice.

13

SPIT IT IN THE BIN

Delivery of a successful lesson is depressingly dependent upon classroom management. My university teaching course ran us through the major discipline styles (which are often called classroom management styles, as discipline has such negative connotations, not to mention S&M overtones). If you are a parent and have ever read a parenting book or blog wondering where you are going wrong with your children, or if you love pop psychology, then the main categories will already be familiar to you. Broadly speaking, the styles are:

• *Authoritarian.* Your teaching style is modelled on Stalin. The classroom is as quiet and productive as a Siberian labour camp. If you are absent for a lesson the students may riot. You often get good results and obedient kids can really like this style of teacher.

• *Authoritative.* You will claim to be this type of teacher as it's the best style (not that there is officially a best style, but this is it). Your teaching style is modelled on Justin Trudeau. You are the iron fist in the velvet glove, softly, softly in charge, responsive to student needs and allowing students to take risks and feel valued even though you're still the boss. The classroom is good-natured and rowdy at times, but none of the kids need therapy afterwards and they keep working away independently even when you leave the classroom pick up something from the printer.

• *Permissive.* You are done with teaching and exerting yourself, as either you are sliding into retirement, or you are younger but still burnt out and just don't give a stuff anymore. You don't have a teaching style and don't really care what the kids do as long as they stay out of your hair and the police don't get called. The class doesn't really respect you, but the feeling is mutual. Many teachers adopt a permissive teaching style on Friday afternoons.

• *Indulgent.* Your teaching style is modelled on how the Coalition government treated the free market. Students can do what they want, when they want, but you still chat to them about it. You take the bus through McDonald's on the school's expense on excursions. You bring in treats all the time. You are the 'Cool Teacher' like Amy Poehler's character of the 'Cool Mom' in *Mean Girls*. The rest of the staffroom have some doubts about you. Sometimes the classroom is noisy, sometimes the kids are all shopping online and it's quiet. The class is often on a tangent. You are a popular teacher, except with Year 12 classes.

It's impossible to assess your own teaching style properly (a bit like assessing how sexy you are in a magazine quiz) but I would say that I started teaching in the Indulgent style, got burnt, tried to be Authoritarian and found it too hard to maintain and then flip-flopped around. Of course, in the same way that you always say you are a good parent but your kids howl with disagreement, it's impossible to claim that you are the very model of an Authoritative teacher.

It's also hard, once a class has got their fix on you, to change your teaching style. There are plenty of teachers who tell newbies the mantra: 'Don't Smile Until Easter.' The class can get to know the real you then, once you've firmly established how scary you are and who is in charge. I am not sure how you develop a relationship with students while this is happening, but I am sure those teachers have quiet, orderly classrooms. There's one other thing I've learnt too: you can't teach if none of the students are listening to you, but just because the class is silent doesn't mean they are actually listening.

Teachers and schools all differ on the classroom rules. Some teachers go ballistic about drink bottles, eating in class or trips to the toilet, while others go gaga on chewing gum and rocking on seats. I've seen an interview where a hard-nosed and highly regarded English English teacher (I've waited decades to type that phrase), recounted how whenever he saw a student tip a chair back onto its rear two legs, he would caution: 'Be careful you don't fall' while swiftly kicking out the stabilising chair legs. While it made me smirk, I'd never have the nerve or, in all honesty, the reflexes to do that.

I heard of one teacher who used to deal with chewing gum by taking the classroom bin to the offender and exhorting the kid to 'spit it in the bin,' and then follow that with the command 'all of it,' often producing a second spit of gum. As someone who likes a discreet chew on a piece of peppermint Extra after lunch so I don't fume teacher coffee breath all over my students, I take a 'don't ask don't tell' approach to gum, and only make it an issue if I can actually hear it being audibly snapped. I'm also a big believer in choosing my battles. I've broadly decided that gum, hair and uniform standards are something for the form teacher who sees that student first thing in the morning to deal with, and not something I need to derail two minutes of the class for during lesson five of the day.

I am, however, driven bats by fidgety kids and would ban clicking-style pens and retractable pencils if I was King of the World, as the clicking during a lesson sends my pulse racing. I have handily diagnosed myself with misophonia (getting unreasonably irritated by certain sounds). If the clicking isn't bothering the students next to the source of the noise, I try to disregard it (and note consolingly that at least the fidgeter is not talking, as otherwise I couldn't hear the clicking).

The noise that makes me enter the ring, spoiling for the fight, is sniffing. I was lucky enough to teach for a while at a school where tissues were included as classroom supplies, and so I could thrust the box of tissues at anyone who dared to sniff without breaking stride. If in a situation with no tissues, I have to send that child to the bathroom to blow their nose. Hey, it's my thing, and I had a primary school teacher with an irrational hatred of the smell of mandarin and used to send us outside to wash our hands if she caught the faintest whiff of citrus, so I'm not the most unreasonable person I've ever heard of (even though that was cold comfort to the hay fever sufferers in my classes).

Managing a classroom is also exhausting because it's part of the emotional labour that most mothers and women in general are familiar with, as you are trying to regulate the emotions of the more than one hundred children you are responsible for each day. When I came home after my first Friday of proper full-time teaching my own classes, I put the television on for my children and went straight to bed. I texted my teaching friends that weekend and no-one answered, as they were all in bed too. It took me absolutely ages to adjust to the exhaustion of always being 'on'. I had done challenging jobs in my twenties and thirties; I'd been the mother of a colicky baby who didn't sleep for more than three hours at a stretch for nine months, but nothing matched the deep in-my-bones exhaustion of that first week of full-time teaching.

When you have a normal job, you are not required to be 'on' all the time. You can sit quietly at your desk for a while just polishing that letter, go to the stockroom or chat to a colleague. When you are teaching, you are always available. You set the emotional weather for the class. It didn't take me long to realise if I was snarly and grumpy (i.e. my natural self) then my classes were filled with sullen students. If I was smiley and cheerful, most of the kids were also in a better mood and the lessons ran more smoothly. Students are always looking at you; your face, your expression, your emotions and your responses are public property. Being calm all day, never swearing or shouting (like you can with your own children) takes a ferocious amount of energy, which must explain why teaching leaves you starving.

It's terrifying that teachers are responsible for some truly astounding things (like their students' behaviour outside, as well as inside, the classroom) and are held to blame when students misbehave, while simultaneously enduring such a low public status. When fights break out at schools, when students are bullied, when school formals go wrong, when young people don't want to work, it's always the fault of their teachers. Unless it is the time for annual best teacher awards, there is never a good news story about teachers in the media or in the comments section on social media. Teachers have a PR reputation equivalent to used car salespeople but with the added bonus of being repeatedly publicly called lazy, communist and academic duds. Teachers are held to a high standard, despite the fact that they are, according to the press and many unkind politicians, 'only teachers' and not paid properly or given the respect they deserve. Badmouthing teachers is an easier (and cheaper) option than fixing the problems facing Australian school children.

It's also unnerving to realise just how much scrutiny you are under as a teacher. Wear a new pair of earrings to school and your class will comment 'new jewellery' while you are still taking attendance. You are a big factor in their lives. In a primary school setting you are a massive influence because you might spend more time with your students during the term than their parents do. If you teach a subject like English or maths at secondary level, that means a lesson every day of the week with each class, and so you still probably see more of your students than most of their parents do. If you have a phobia about, say, sniffing, you have five days a week, forty weeks a year to impose your quirks on your class. If you hate kids saying 'like' or neglecting to say 'please' then you've got ample time to bend them to your will (or at least, expose then to another viewpoint).

Teachers are also under scrutiny outside the classroom. If you live in the same local area you teach in, you face judgement whenever you leave the house from students, former students and parents and grandparents of your students and former students. These people can add up to almost your entire local community. This is the reason why plenty of teachers choose to teach somewhere that's a good long commute from home. It's also a reason why some teachers don't want to work in the country, where it's even harder to escape from the community.

The scrutiny covers what you are wearing, what you are doing, and most challenging of all, how you are parenting. Wearing Ugg boots and a vintage tracksuit to the newsagent, laughing loudly with your pals at the pub, arguing with your children in a department store on the incredibly 'rare' times that you have to disagree with them, and buying all of the Pizza Shapes and none of the fresh fruit in the supermarket are all moments that leave you open to 'guess what I saw?' conversations among your school-related network.

It is also (and I do understand this as I used to suffer from it myself before I became a teacher) deeply unsettling to see one of your former – or even worse – your current teachers, walking around in your space JUST LIKE A NORMAL PERSON. It's like seeing a dragon, an actor or a minor Royal as part of your everyday: part shock, part revulsion and part fascination. As a student, you want your teacher to be present in 'teacher mode' at school, and then go live in a box somewhere (maybe doing their marking) until they reappear in the classroom. It can make students feel vaguely queasy and unreal when teachers talk about their life at home, or when they see them driving into school. Even I, as a grown woman and a teacher myself, struggle to address my former teachers by their first names, defaulting to their courtesy titles of Mrs So and So.

Teachers, in order to do their job, have to project an aura of 'the good teacher', which is part control, part role play and lots of hard work. I used to refer to my 'teacher clothes' and my 'teacher voice' as part of that package. The classroom discipline that teachers employ every day is one reason why an appearance outside the classroom seems so unsettling. Students are rightfully spooked when they see you blinking in the daylight outside of the school grounds as they can clearly remember that just hours ago you were chastising them for laziness, telling them they talk too much and firmly advising them to work on their personal organisation skills.

A whole lot of classroom management is basically imposing simple manners and polite behaviour on a class (listen to others, one person speaks at a time, be kind). Once you have been doing it long enough, you might find some weird aspects to classroom management that start to loom large in your life. The thing I really struggled with was getting students in the last lesson of the day to put their chairs up on their desks. For my first term of my proper teaching job, the bell would ring for the end of the day, and whatever class I had would frenziedly throw their gear together and race for the door, while I pleaded 'Stop, the class isn't over, come back and put up your chairs,' to an empty classroom. Then, like the sap, I am, I would tour the classroom dutifully putting up all the chairs.

I've been very spoiled with the schools I have taught in, but other teachers had horror stories of knives and punches being thrown, or of students crawling out of the windows to drop from a second-floor balcony. My classroom discipline could, once I had been blooded and had my hard stare sorted after my first two years, mostly be managed with a 'settle down' and a threat to call the student's parents in for a chat. In my first few years of teaching, I found the toughest thing to manage was disciplining a student in the classroom during the lesson.

Even though in TV series set in schools, students who misbehave are sent 'straight to the principal's office' (even in the show *Sex Education*), in the private sector it's an unspoken rule that sending a student you can't manage to the Principal or Vice Principal is like sending in your own resignation letter, all in capital letters, saying 'I CAN'T DO MY JOB'. Essentially, they are your students, your problem, so you must cope on your own.

In my second teaching placement, my kind and capable supervising teacher had to rear up from her seat and take command of a rampaging Year 9 class which had become out of control. She brushed away my gibbering thanks when we were in the hallway after the lesson. I was left with a well-founded dread of Year 9 and sinking feeling that I would never make it. I worried that I lacked the essential attributes of a teacher. Like the depressing saying went, teachers are born, not made. Maybe, I worried, I just didn't have it? The supervising teacher generously told me that I did have it, but I had my doubts.

To my mind, a good teacher has the following personality traits, skills and characteristics.

• The ability to write neatly and evenly on a whiteboard. Their letters do not get smaller and smaller as they write, and their sentences do not slope away to the right-hand side of the board, as happens to normal people. They can write legible comments on students' work. I was an abject failure at both of those things. My students would hold back from criticising my messy writing on the white board as they knew that if they did, I'd get them up the front of the classroom with a whiteboard marker 'to be my scribe'. Putting a classical, Ancient Roman Empire spin on anything can justify a lot, right up to slavery.

• Excellent spelling. When students are calling out suggestions and you are putting it all up on the board, you need to know how to spell everything instinctively. Write up a misspelling and some kid may take a photo on their smart phone, laptop or iPad and circulate it widely. I am always uncertain about how to spell 'onomatopoeia' and used to have to confess that failing to my English students rather than be exposed by my dodgy spelling. (You know onomatopoeia, it's when words evoke the actual sound, like the BAM, BANG and ticking sounds that are beloved of comic strips and poetry.) I used to rather evilly suggest that if students were not confident of how to spell a word, such as onomatopoeia, that they maybe wrote that word a little untidily accidentally on purpose in their English exam papers. Exam technique is a big part of successful exam taking. It's all a game. I used to say, just give the markers what they want. And if you do nothing else, make the final sentence of your essay so profound and insightful that the examiner, who is always most taken by the last thing they have read, feels compelled to give you an A.

• They tell other people, even ones they don't know, to be quiet, pick up that piece of rubbish and stand over there. Just as a room of lawyers is a room full of different opinions, a room of teachers is a room of people who all want to take charge and tell everyone what to do. As a teaching friend used to say to me whenever there was an incident at a school that required direction: 'Just hold back, one of the staff will tell us what to do any moment now.'

• They like stationery, colour-coded files and small admin. They love to go wild in Officeworks with their own money in the summer holidays, buying colour-coded Post-it notes and folders. Year 9 will be green, Year 10 yellow and they will have all the stationery to match. They love folders. Even in an online school with electronic assessments, teachers will have a gorgeous hard copy folder for each class. The older the teacher, the more folders they have neatly arranged down the side of their desk. Much like counting rings in a tree, you can count the number of ring-bound folders in the workroom as a proxy calculation of a teacher's age.

• They like to hold the floor. Every lesson is a mini performance to a captive audience, which is probably the true appeal of teaching for many people. This is my purest teacher characteristic, as I can babble on continuously unless stopped at gunpoint.

• They are good with names. One of my teacher friends boasts that she can get a class of twenty-five unknown students with names matched to faces before the first lesson is over, and she isn't exaggerating. It's one of the many intimidatingly capable things about her. I still don't have all the names to faces of the girls who were in my own year at school.

• They have a scary, dead-eyed smile that makes children unwillingly do things they don't want to do, a matching teacher voice with the same chilling nature and the ability to clear a hip city nightspot just by arriving and being seen by the kids at the bar.

• They are, at heart, good people who want to help others and to make the world a better place. They spend hours listening to their students' problems, they run charity drives in their spare time and they buy things that their students need out of their own pay. I hope I have made it clear as you read this that I am no longer a teacher.

In my first proper teaching job, I struggled with classroom management with all my classes, but especially my Year 9 classes. If I was a second late to the classroom, there would be almost a riot taking place by the time I walked in. The class kept talking over me, wrestling with each other in their seats and were so noisy and boisterous that we couldn't do any 'fun' (that's teacher fun, not real fun) group activities as everyone would be off task in less than a minute. I started having a sinking feeling before their lessons. Like the super emotional perception attributed to dogs and other wild animals, these children could sense my fear and got worse and worse as the weeks went on. One day after I had confided in a kind and experienced teacher who had a lesson timetabled in the neighbouring classroom to mine, he came in and blew his stack at the kids when he heard them acting up in my lesson. The class was subdued for the next few days, but it was still mortifying that the students would settle down for him, and not for me.

The main issue was with a few rowdy ringleaders in this class. I am terrible at remembering peoples' names, but of course knew the names of these students by the end of our first lesson. When fellow students keep calling out, 'Oh Little Johnny you are so naughty,' admiringly, you quickly learn who Little Johnny is. Sometimes, I would resort to sending Little Johnny to the front office with the roll call record, lying that the internet was down, just so I could have a quieter five minutes to run through my planned lesson outline with the class. He always came back, eventually, which was quite disappointing. He was not a delinquent; he just really had my number.

I had many chats with Little Johnny, one on one. When the lesson was before lunch or recess, or the last lesson of the day, I could keep him back for a 'discussion', but when the class ran into another lesson I'd have to take him out into the hallway for a half-whispered dressing down. None of these chats had any effect at all. I honestly don't know if my classroom management improved in later years, or whether I just was super lucky never to have a Little Johnny darken my class lists again.

PE
teachers
love good
sports

14

FUN AND GAMES

Towards the end of the first (summer) term of my first proper year as a teacher, I encountered that Australian sporting rite of passage: swimming sports day. Actual sport sports day, with sneakers, running and athletic events, is usually held in a later, winter term, when staff and students can get thoroughly rained upon and all catch colds before the mid-year exams. Swimming sports day is held earlier, when it's still hot.

The first sign of swimming sports day was the unwelcome notice and email that I was to spend my precious lunch times for a week, and more time after school, supervising and timing swimming trials in the school pool. You would think that the PE Department would hand out supervision rosters to the newest and least sporty members of staff for some fun stuff not associated with swimming. Of course not. Instead, I found myself overpowered by the PE staff and, in turn admiring the bravery of teenagers. As if being a teenager, having to come to school daily, and do battle with your hormones, and your parents, wasn't enough, you also have to wear school bathers in front of your peers. Plenty of adults I know won't do this, so my admiration for courageous young people of Australia is boundless. School bathers are always epically unflattering, with an uncanny ability to give a wedgie and simultaneously fail to support any bulges.

Shepherding the girls in my class to and from their swimming trials also meant I had to develop a strategy for changing rooms (mine was to stand outside the entrance door bellowing 'Hurry up,' like I was Blackboard in *Mr Squiggle*, and to ban the use of spray deodorant as it would invariably set of the school smoke alarm or trigger an asthma attack).

When we finally made it to the pool, I discovered the stopwatch. It looked simple but had two different buttons and I would unerringly press the wrong one every single race. If I managed to press the right one I pressed it too late. Or not press it hard enough, so the poor kid would be halfway down the pool by the time that I belatedly noticed that my stopwatch was still at 00:00:00. Timekeeping also turns out to be one of those deceptively challenging tasks that requires the ability to concentrate on the sport all the time. I could not maintain focus even for a thirty-six-second race and was invariably gazing blankly into middle distance by the time the poor swimmer in my lane put their hand (in a regulation swimming-approved manner, I hoped, but not that I was looking in the right direction at the right time) at the end of the pool. Normally, the PE teacher in charge had marked down the top three swimmers anyway on their ever-present clipboard, so my incompetence did not really matter, and I promised hollowly that I'd have it all sorted by the big day.

The big day involved dressing in my house colours (I can't remember the name of the English writer who snidely observed that feeling loyalty to one's school assigned house was akin to feeling loyalty to one's prison, but of course I agree with such a cynical sentiment), and then arriving at school to oversee the explosion of house patriotism. In defiance of the notes I had sent home with my form, students were covered with hair spray, glitter, makeup and what I hoped were temporary tattoos in their house colours. They were filled with boisterous cheer at the prospect of a day without lessons and happily shouted their house chants (the best sounded like they were rude, but cunningly weren't really, and just caused the Head of House to choke on their coffee each time they started up) while I tried to take attendance. We then went out and queued for the hired buses for the trip to the Olympic-sized pool.

This was virtually an excursion. You have to really love admin (or teach geography or drama) to put up with the hassle of all the paperwork involved organising an excursion. At many schools you must prepare a plan which is submitted to the Deputy Head at least four weeks in advance, outlining: why you want to go; when you want to go; what lessons and school events the students will miss while they are going; the costs; an assessment of the health and safety risks, and a discussion of how you will meet the student /teacher ratios.

(This is the only time having a student teacher is useful, as you can rope them in to make up your numbers.) Obviously no-one wants a student to die under their care, so I do understand the health and safety concerns, however, when you teach something as lame as English, and are taking a class to see a play in a theatre, and you have to write 'a student may choke on a Jaffa' as a potential risk, you do wonder whether the school lawyers could have two sorts of forms: one for high-risk and one for low-risk excursions. Then you have to book the transport, write and send out the consent forms, gather and keep track of the consent forms, email follow-ups to the usual suspects about returning consent forms and invariably phone one parent on the day and beg them to please sign the form.

The school nurse prepares a first aid list for you and, as a responsible teacher, you will be handed a special first aid kit for each child with an allergy, asthma, diabetes or any other medical issue. Usually you have less first aid kits than students, but I'm sure that might change in the future. Then the day before the excursion, you triple check the consent forms, gather the first aid kits and give the class a pep talk about uniform standards and 'representing the school'. Once the day arrives and you have heaved the first aid trunk, your class list and your excursion notes onto the bus, you can begin the fun of counting heads. To lose a student on an excursion is the ultimate faux pas, and so you count heads (sometimes even touching the heads if you have been recently spooked by *Home Alone*), every time the kids move. You count them on the bus, off the bus, when you walk anywhere, when you arrive anywhere and after they go to the toilet. You are keyed up with responsibility until you safely count them all off the bus when you finally arrive back at school. Your friends will never enjoy going on a winery tour or hen's party minibus trip with you ever again, as you will be compelled to loudly and annoying headcount people all day. They put up with a lot being friends with a teacher anyway, the whingeing about marking, the tiredness, the inability to speak on the phone after a school day, and so the headcount bossiness is yet another cross to bear and a good reason why teachers often just socialise with other teachers. The one plus of being tall is that it was easy to fix a spot for my students to meet me if they got lost somewhere in the foyer of the theatre. 'You can always find me in a crowd. If you get lost, meet at Mrs Brooks.'

For the school swimming carnival, the PE Department had handled a lot of this red tape, and the school nurse was coming with us, so I only needed to headcount my own class onto the bus and then sit with them on the way there and headcount them off the bus, before starting my supervision duties. The day had been divided into exciting segments of different chores, none of which entailed academic instruction, but several which involved life skills I did not possess.

Presumably due to my rock bottom status as one of the newest members of staff, I had to commence the day with responsibility for supervising the girls' bathroom and changerooms. Just like Moaning Myrtle from *Harry Potter*. It's hard to sit in a changing room without looking unbelievably (and probably illegally) creepy, so I settled for random, short and brisk inspections, making sure no-one was smoking, using their phone or tormenting their peers. In between I just sat outside the door enjoying the smell of chlorine in the air and the carnival atmosphere.

After a few hours, my 'duty roster' changed to a scheduled break, and so I crept out into the light and the humidity of the crowded tiered seating overlooking the pool. Students were cheering, screaming and eating vast quantities of sweets, most cheerfully disregarding the anonymous swimmers, whose hideously unflattering bather outfits were now topped off by colourful swimming caps, racing away in the pool below. I found some of my teaching pals tucked away high in the tiered seating and settled in for a gossip, delighted to have some almost free time. I tried not to think about the mound of marking I still needed to do before school tomorrow.

I spent an enjoyable ten minutes hearing all about one of the younger staff member's latest dating exploits, and helped her review the latest offerings on Tinder. Intermittently I had to be responsible, occasionally sending students who came up for help with mild injuries to the school nurse, who had set up camp near the commentary box. Despite these interruptions, we were just settling down to discuss whether men who couldn't button their shirts up in their profile pictures were always a no, when a shadow fell over me and I felt a chill. I looked up to see a member of the PE Department looming over me. He was, like all the PE staff, dressed in the usual school PE staff uniform, rather than wearing colours to show allegiance to a particular house. He was, I noticed, looking cool and calm despite the high humidity. I was dripping in sweat and you could have steamed a dumpling under my dress.

'Georgie,' he said. I was secretly embarrassed that he knew my name. I still couldn't tell the PE staff apart yet. I peered myopically at his name badge but gave up.

'Yes darling,' I said, pathetically, taking refuge in the phrasing of the demented middle-aged woman he no doubt thought I was.

'You're on the back-up list.' Of course I was. 'One of the timekeepers has twisted her ankle on the edge of the pool, so you're it,' he informed me, and then without waiting for discussion, headed down the stairs.

'Thanks to injury, my selection has come up,' I joked to my friend, and then I pulled myself up from the sticky plastic seat and weaved my way down from the anonymity of the stands.

On the way I told two separate and unknown students to pick up their ice block wrappers and put them in the bin, so I was internally congratulating myself that I was a proper teacher. Then I reached the edge of the pool and my confidence took a dive. It looked depressingly professional, with students patiently queueing for their races, a huge scoreboard and even a gun for the race starts. The PE staff member who had rounded me up from the stands told me briskly that I was on for the next race, there was no time to waste. I was shepherded in at the end of lane five and handed a huge black stopwatch. It was on a string, which the PE teacher looped around my wrist. 'So, you don't drop it in the pool' he explained, clearly anticipating how clumsy I was.

'Now here's the button to start,' he said with a wave. 'And this one has a separate stop button,' he continued, with another wave. I looked at the stopwatch. It had four buttons. The stopwatch I'd failed to use properly at the school swimming trials had just two. The PE teacher was already walking away, and my fellow teachers had stepped up to their marks. I moved onto the high concrete edge of the pool, almost overbalanced and fell in, then corrected myself. How the hell had I ended up spending a random Thursday doing this?

The gun sounded and I nervously hit what I really hoped was the correct button. It wasn't, I had somehow gone into another page on the screen. I pressed another button, and a timer started clicking. If the kid in my lane was going to get a place, my incompetence would be revealed and I might ruin it for them. Was there no end to the harm I could do to young lives by my teaching? I anxiously scanned the pool. The kid in my lane was coming second to last. Excellent news. I kept looking and yep, they were the aquatic equivalent of me. Fortunately, they finished still second to last. I bent down to the end of the pool to congratulate them. 'A great swim,' I said warmly. 'You came seventh. It was a tough race.' The student pulled up their goggles and smiled sweetly at me. 'Thanks Miss,' he said. At that moment I was filled with the warm glow of doing what I loved. While officious waiters had been calling me 'madam' for decades now, the standard default student form of address for any female teacher was 'Miss'. It still gave me a small thrill, even though it was usually in the irritating context of 'Miss, I really don't know what happened to the assignment. I promise it was on my laptop last night.'

The PE staff only took the times for the top three placegetters, so my incompetence was masked for the moment. I focused intently, and by keeping my finger on the correct button, managed to correctly time the next group of races. There was then a small break while the next event queued up and I began chatting to the teacher next to me. Completely distracted, I missed the start of the next race and only hit the button when I saw my fellow teacher do it correctly. 'I missed the start,' I confessed. 'What's your time?' He told me, and I admitted that I was terrible at timekeeping.

'Must be a mistake,' he said. 'Usually they only let you dreamy English teachers hand out the ribbons.' I almost felt a surge of professional pride and bumbled on for another hour until another teacher came to relive me from my post.

Stepping away from the pool, desperate to go the loo and to splash cold water on my face, I was corralled by an anxious student who wanted to discuss why they hadn't got an A on their latest assignment. As I was on my way to start my next stint of changeroom supervision, I asked the student to walk and talk with me. A fact of teaching is that while you have many students, they only have a handful of teachers, and you need to project the nurturing air that their wellbeing is your sole and top focus at all times. This means you need to be ready to discuss the intricacies of the best essay question to choose if maybe 'one hasn't, theoretically of course, finished the novel' with a random Year 10 while you do yard duty. It means you need to be able to recall everything about that student, their work so far, their home life, how they have been doing in their past formative assessments, whenever and wherever you see them, no matter how off-putting the context.

A lot of modern teaching is justifying the mark you have given (to the student and sometimes to their parents as well). It makes me nostalgic for my own youth, and jealous of how good my teachers had it. They couldn't be emailed by parents out of hours (or at any time at all), their word was law, no kid could record the lesson or take a photo without dragging in a huge bulky piece of equipment, and parents at home always backed them up. One of my own teachers was infamous for his re-marking. If you ever queried a grade, he would take the work back from you and state that he would give you that extra mark, but only once he'd looked through the work again and found somewhere that you needed to lose another mark. Of course, no-one ever asked for a re-mark.

It's a difficult fact that marking artsy subjects is invariably subjective. While there's often a right or wrong in maths (and the hope of showing some excellent working out along the way), in English once you have looked at the spelling, the use of grammar, the correct form, the use of appropriate supporting quotations from the text, you are left making a subjective assessment about the quality of the student's literary analysis, and there is no right or wrong. This uncertainty, the shades of grey, are one of things I love most about teaching English, but I do appreciate for those craving certainty that this must be infuriating.

Sometimes when I'd say to my students, 'there is no right

answer here, marshal the evidence and create a beautifully written argument,' they would look agitated. Surely, I was joking again? There is a common band of consensus amongst English teachers, and normally we can agree about the grade to give. Most schools encourage 'cross marking', where all the English teachers separately mark the same pieces of work and note what grade they would give and why, to ensure you are all on the same page regarding As, Bs etc. It's always surprisingly stressful, but a relief once it is done, when you are reassured that you are all on the same page. However, even when on the same page, you are not necessarily on the same paragraph. That elusive half grade, the thing that turns an A into an A plus is where the magic and the disagreements happen. Eventually, if you get fed up with it, you will have to become head of the faculty so you can make the line calls in the event of a difference of opinion between two passionate members of staff. There's always wiggle room, and a different argument that might just change your mind and the grade.

I'm talking here about the finicky hard stuff. Most marking isn't that contentious, it's just immensely time consuming. When you really get your eye in, you can often know 'in your waters' whether you are you looking at an A, B, C or, Lord help me, a D, from the opening paragraph. One of the real disappointments for me in my teaching career was that although my marking got faster as I became more experienced, I reached a dead end where no further time improvement was possible, and I still had hours upon hours of marking to do every week.

I've left the full-bore whingeing about marking for as

long as I can – it's been what I'd call just a dull whine up to now (and I've even smuggled it into a chapter ostensibly about swimming sports day) – because I know, after bitter experience, that everyone is sick to the back teeth of teachers complaining about all their marking. But we are only repeating ourselves it because it's true. And there are lots of types of teachers that even I don't want to hear whingeing about their marking (just how time consuming are those multiple-choice tests?) But for senior school teachers of language-rich subjects, I feel your pain and I'm going to howl for us all.

Marking takes aeons of time, and you have to concentrate while you do it, so you can't be multi-tasking, or listening to someone or something else. Even when you are an experienced teacher, you often have to recalibrate after the first few assignments from the same class and go back and reassess the first ones from the batch to confirm that you have been fair, and that the students have a handle on the task. In my first year of teaching I used to run through and reconsider each and every assignment again and my initial grade once I had done the lot. However, now I'm more like a pancake chef, and just anxiously re-check the first few that are often unreliable while the pan is still getting hot (easy, lazy simile, with no reference to the subject matter and no deep insight: mark it down).

Marking a long senior essay or assignment also takes time, regardless of your level of skill and experience. A Year 12 essay can be 1000 words long, and a Year 11 essay 800 words long. If I was on fire, caffeinated and all was well, it would still take a minimum of thirty minutes to mark each essay, record the grade and add some pithy notes in my mark book or laptop. If you are writing helpful, constructive feedback (and as a good teacher you are of course doing this) it will take time, lots of precious time, to mark each essay. The feedback is where it is all at, as it's the individualised attention that helps the student improve and shows that you care. It's really challenging to do it properly. You want to be constructive, you want to make suggestions, and you really want to stop writing about apostrophe usage by the second page. If you have twenty-five students in your class (and that is standard), the absolute best-case scenario is that it will therefore take you twelve and a half hours as a minimum (allowing thirty minutes for each) to mark all the essays in your pile for that class. That is twelve and a half hours of marking on top of your teaching, your lesson planning, your yard duty, your co-curricular supervision, your pastoral care of your students, and your one-on-one sessions with students to help them with a particular assignment. In secondary English, most courses have seven big ticket summative   assignments per year, so that is a mountain of marking to do (plus you may want to set some formative work for marking as well). Sure, you can get it all done, but something's got to give.

The 'crowning turd in the waterpipe' (thank you *Blackadder*) for language-rich subject teachers has been the insidious introduction of the 'draft'. This is the idea that for Year 12 subjects (some schools like teachers to do it for Year 11 students as well, but honestly, resign while you still have the strength if that happens), students get to submit a draft version of each assignment for marking and feedback before they submit the final version. Marking a draft takes even longer than marking the final piece, as you are trying to stretch the student and provide feedback (but not spoon-feed them) about how they can make the work better. The concept of drafts, at a single stroke, doubled the workload of most Year 12 teachers.

Rumour has it that teachers at some private schools will even take in a second or a third draft from a student. This is not only strictly forbidden (apparently all's fair in love, war and the pursuit of a good ATAR) but it's also bad for the student's own academic development and ownership of their work. More importantly it is BLOODY NUTS. I have no idea how any teacher could find the time to squeeze in another round of drafts, or even want to do so.

As the good teacher I was trying to be, I stopped on my way to the bathroom and earnestly discussed the student's concerns with her. I quoted from my earlier comments on her assignment. I told her that she couldn't re-submit it, but that I looked forward to her next piece of work. I told her that she had shown a good grasp of the concepts, and that her writing style was clear and fluent. I told her that an A minus was really a very good grade.

Then I went to the bathroom and blessedly splashed water on my face. So cool, and even better, the day was already more than halfway over. I heard a commotion, and then a group of girls came running in to me.

'Miss, Miss,' they said. 'Come into the change rooms. Mr A from the PE department said he can't possibly come into the girls' change rooms.'

'What is it?' I asked, anxious that I did not have my trusty first aid box to hand.

'It's Susie, she's so sick.'

And she had been. Susie, by the looks of the contents of her stomach, was in the blue house, and had eaten what looked like five kilograms worth of blue sweets. Her stomach had, unsurprisingly, rebelled and there was house-loyal vomit as far as the eye could see.

'Gross,' groaned her peers, retreating and leaving me to it.

'It's okay Susie,' I said. 'Did you feel a bit off colour this morning?' I was trying desperately to avoid a gag about feeling blue.

'Girls,' I screeched. 'Get a female PE teacher in here to help me.'

15

LET ME TELL YOU WHAT
I REALLY THINK

Towards the end of my first proper year of teaching, the school year and calendar seemed to move even faster. Exams were required to be set at warp speed and then marked on the run so the feedback could be incorporated into the school reports. My children had their own exciting schedule of end-of-year activities which also ate into my marking time.

I lovingly watched my son perform in his supporting role of 'Half the Camel' in his school nativity play, and felt wracked with jealousy at the primary school teachers who only had twenty-five school reports to write. No wonder they were all so young and pretty and had such magnificent hair. I had 125 reports to write and only 123 left to finish in the year that was rapidly receding in the rear windscreen. We celebrated my son's successful performance with a dinner out at the pub, while my marking sat in the car but still making me feel bad from a distance. Unmarked marking is pretty powerful. It's a sort of mind and mood control device. After dinner, tucking the children into their beds and putting on a load of washing so the camel suit could go back to school, I sat down to try and write some more of my reports.

I asked one of my friends from the staffroom if he could read my first report just to check if it was okay. There was a style guide to follow, but like every style guide ever written, it was so boring that you instantly forgot what you had read while you were still reading it. I had to write 200 words for each of my English students, and 400 words for the students in my form group.

The school was conscious that parents were customers, and so it was keen to make the report an uplifting experience. Where possible, shortcomings had to be described in a positive manner. This was not only kind, but sensible, as I could still remember my own primary school report that accurately described me as dreamy and bad at maths. It's so easy for a report to become a self-fulfilling prophecy. There's no doubt that reports were harsher in the past and included withering assessments of the life potential of a student. This does, of course, provide some amusement when the predication in the report fails to come true, like Albert Einstein's 1895 school report that reputedly said (although presumably it said so in German) that 'he will never amount to anything'. I can't imagine ever wanting to predict anything like that for a student. No-one wants to provide or read a life forecast for students anymore. Reports are meant to be more actual report, less speculation and character assassination, although there's no doubt that they are less fun to read than they used to be. If you genuinely were going to deliver awful news in a report, teachers were told that they had to phone the parents in advance so that the dire grades could be discussed, and hopefully defused, before the report hand grenade was lobbed.

Fortunately, the wonders of modern technology meant that I could write my reports at home, and no parents needed to be exposed to just how terrible my handwriting really was. One experienced teacher had told me that when she started, reports were written in little booklets that were all laid out on tables in a central room, and teachers had to stay at school each night to neatly write their comments on each report. Left-handed teachers apparently lived in horror of smudging the ink and making everyone stay back and re-write the report. Now I could sit at my kitchen table and work, and also hang my washing out when I needed to. (A cynical part of me also thinks that it's easier for systems to turn a blind eye to how much work goes into report writing when the teachers are doing that work privately at home, rather than publicly at school.) Every single person in the staffroom also took me aside to warn me to write my report comments separately and save them on a word document, as they all had remembered times when the school's report programme had crashed and lost all their comments. Older teachers had some phrases they could trot out each year and their own Homeric epithets to apply to each situation. Such is the nature of teaching – the classes change, but the types of kids do not. There is often a rumour going around that some tech savvy member of staff has cracked the questionable goal of automatic computer-generated reports. There is so much repetition in reports that it does seem like it might be feasible for some, with only the need for a short and personalised comment to be added. A counter-swirling rumour often circulates that the school management can detect 'cut and paste' jobs in reports.

My sample report comment passed muster, but my unofficial mentor noticed my tendency to humour and firmly told me that reports were not the place to be funny. This was a little disappointing, as I had always wanted to emulate my grandfather John, who retold with pride his story of the cleverest reference he ever wrote. My grandfather was a farmer and had a succession of jackaroos work for him to help with the cattle and the sheep. The jackaroos worked with him every day, ate every meal in his house (my grandmother retired from cooking when they left the farm) and when they moved on to their next job, expected my grandfather to write a reference for them on his good notepaper (engraved with the name of the property and its Private Mail Bag number) which they would take with them to their next job. The jackaroos would all obviously read the reference themselves and probably have read it before they left the farm.

My grandfather had dealt with a difficult life by developing the most impeccable manners, and he was known in his social set as 'Gentleman John'. He had been a soldier in the Australian Army and had fabulous mementos including the samurai sword 'given' to him by a Japanese soldier. He could also give a 'martial' bellow to his sons. At one stage, my grandfather had working for him one of the most lazy and incompetent men he had ever met. Eventually, this jackaroo took the hint and decided to move on, but not before he asked my grandfather for a reference. After much thought (and presumably deep consideration in his study, where my grandfather paid the farm accounts and battled the 'paper war') he produced the reference, which said that Mr Useless had been employed by him during the following dates. This was followed by the clincher, 'if you can get him to work for you, you are a lucky man.' Apparently the jackaroo had ridden away, entirely happy with this back-handed compliment.

A few favourites from the staffroom were 'makes a lively contribution to class' (never stops talking), 'is shy and reserved' (never speaks in class), 'is a deep thinker' (never speaks and never does any of the allocated tasks), 'needs to work on their organisational skills' (always late with their work), 'has a vivid imagination' (a fantasist), 'a socially vivacious member of the class' (sometimes can be the leader of the bitch pack) and 'needs to learn how to work independently' (I want you to stop doing your child's homework).

But my reports weren't all euphemism and mirrors. Particularly for the children who tried and were underappreciated, I ensured that I provided a truthful, if unacademic, response to their efforts. My reports were permitted to include my honest favourable opinions: 'Sally is a charming and polite student', 'Riyash tries hard and always gives his best effort', 'Sophie's sense of humour enlivens all of our lessons', 'the class is a better place with Chu in it'. It was feedback of a sort, and probably the kind of thing that would linger in the subconscious long after 'Thomas has excellent skills in using evidence from the texts but needs to ensure his work is carefully edited'.

My school reports not only had to include the comments and a grade, but we had to also assign a value for 'effort'. This was intangible, something that couldn't be tracked thorough centralised testing or ranked via NAPLAN. I felt liberated by being able to hand out a score without doing some complex (to me) calculations. After I completed all the reports, I finally realised that I was using the effort grade as a proxy for how much I personally liked the student. I asked around in the staffroom if anyone else did that and was almost drowned in a stern wave of disapproval. It was as if I'd asked them to name their favourite child. It was a taboo. Everyone pontificated at length (and no-one pontificates as much as teachers in an Arts faculty) at the arcane systems they had in place for determining the score for each student. They spoke of the homework completed on time, the independent thought, the participation in class discussions, the honesty and the helpfulness of the students. I got it. Subtext and all that. Everyone was handing out the effort score based on how much they liked that student.

I finally completed my reports and survived the process of incorporating the proofreader's comments. These were distributed to us in our staff pigeonholes as pencil scrawls made by an unknown editor on a print-out. We had one working day to incorporate the edits. In a manner that probably explained why the English teachers had been placed in a staffroom on their own, we were all unable to accept the edits without some questioning. 'It's grammatically incorrect', 'it has no flair', and 'it has ruined the rhythm of my sentence' were all comments made out loud, to the murmured agreement of our peers, as we took the executive decision not to make the mandated edits.

'Will I get into trouble for not making my edits?' I nervously asked my mentor. (Once a nerdy anxious teacher's pet, always a nerdy anxious teacher's pet.)

'Don't worry,' came the reassuring reply. 'Even management are under the pump at this time of year. They can't check all the edits, and so only the reports by the maths and PE department will get a double check.'

World's
best
teacher.

16

IT'S THE MOST WONDERFUL TIME OF THE YEAR

The school campus seems eerily empty for the last few weeks of the school year as the Year 12s always leave school after their final exams and these finish well before the end of term. The Year 11s start peacocking around, already planning how they will consolidate their hold on the best spots in the yard next year. They all want anxious one-on-one meetings with you to finalise their subject choices for Year 12, and you are suddenly an unwilling font of knowledge, with a grasp on the subject prerequisites for almost every course in Australia.

There's normally a last-day-of-school show of some sort (Covid willing), where you turn up and watch awe-struck as the music department coax magical harmonies out of the most unlikely students. You try to forget about your radioactive pile of marking and make chitchat to anxious parents and relaxed students. The staff of the music department leave the show draped in glitter and head out for drinks, while you go home and try to remember why you didn't finish your marking earlier.

An near delirium sweeps the school on the last day. Everyone is cheerful and relaxed. Classes are chatty and excitable, attributable to the upcoming long holidays and the dozens of candy canes they have eaten by recess time. Teachers are meant to supervise locker cleaning, and the whole class will squeal with delight and horror when someone unearths a green sandwich and liquified black banana leftover from Term 2. There is a final assembly, with a blessed lack of upcoming notices, and the loudest singing that has been heard all year.

At the end of my first year, on the advice of my mentor teacher, I asked my classes to provide feedback on their time with me in English. They delightedly and honestly joined in, once I had confirmed that yes, their reports were all done and locked up in the front office.

Some of them confessed that they had never finished the novel we had studied, and a few brave souls admitted that they had never even started it. They had enjoyed a surprising amount of the course, with the exception of grammar and the exams. One lovely child said that she would like to be an English teacher when she grew up, and I handed her one of my secret stash of red frogs – the allergy-aware treat I kept in my work bag to bribe and or reward outstanding work.

We relived the best in-jokes of the year: the time I had projected the inbox from my personal email onto the class whiteboard; the time I was impersonating a barking dog when the head master was leading a school tour of prospective parents and the time that a student had started crying in class when I was explaining euphemisms (a surprisingly hard lesson to teach, with wholesome student-suitable euphuisms a challenge to find) and I had written 'our dog has gone to live on the farm' on the board, and then had explained what had really happened to the dog. That poor student had still not twigged, until Mrs Brooks actually taught her something new that day: her old dog was not currently living out his best life on a farm.

We then had a final form session for the year. I gave each student a candy cane and told them what I had learnt from each of them. I then, after some suspicious rustling, was given chocolates, mugs and a posy of flowers from some of the students. Each of these presents came with a handwritten card, which made it all the more heartfelt because I didn't need to mark them. My favourite card simply said, 'Mrs Brooks, I have enjoyed English this year and I never thought I would.' I started to cry, then fortunately the final bell for the year rang.

The class ran outside, selectively deaf, and aware of my new powerlessness.

'Come back,' I bellowed. 'I haven't dismissed you. And you need to put the chairs up.'

One student turned around for a farewell wave, and then rounded the corner and was gone. My first proper class. I picked up all the plastic wrappers from the candy canes, put them in the bin, and then dutifully put up all the chairs.

EXTENSION ACTIVITIES
FOR SPECIAL CREDIT

Q1. The author says that there are no correct answers in English. Is this true? Select one answer only.

a)   Yes
b)   No
c)   Maybe
d)   It depends upon how fluently you explain your position.

Q2. Which of the following responses best captures the author's opinion about marking?

a)   Favourable
b)   Unfavourable
c)   Boringly laboured and repetitive.
d)   I don't know as I skipped those bits – they were like the endless pointless Elf songs in *Lord of the Rings*.

Q3. Memoirs are written in the first person, using the pronoun 'I'. Which of the common limitations of the first person outlined below did you find most irritating in the text?

a)   It portrayed the point of view of only one person (and quite a dull person at that).
b)   The first-person point of view is inherently biased and limited, and especially so here because of the author herself.
c)   The diction used by the author is restricted, and additionally contains too much bloody swearing, unnecessary teaching, pedagogical jargon and lame-ass colloquialisms.
d)   The repetitive use of 'I think' is redundant (not to mention annoying) as it's obvious that the text portrays a subjective viewpoint.

Q4. Grammar is important. It is the difference between helping your Uncle Jack off a horse, and helping your uncle jack off a horse. Similarly, and less smuttily, I like eating pets and family is much less troubling when commas are used to clarify that I like eating, pets and family. The text demonstrated many idiosyncratic ways in which the author uses grammar. Which of the following did you find the most distressing?

a) The author used far (and I really mean this) too many brackets.

b) The author, who claimed to be an English teacher, failed to defend the rule against split infinitives, and I am only at the end of the book to try and find details of her publisher so I can write them a strongly-worded letter of complaint.

c) The author and the editor have differing views about the use of the Oxford comma. Confusingly, it could have been used in many more chapters, and examples, and anecdotes, and even this quiz.

d) The author claimed that grammar lessons could be used as a threat to subdue a classroom.

Self-reflection task

This memoir contains many (heavily fictionalised) stories from the author's time as a teacher, with a humorous focus on moments where the author failed to achieve the best outcomes for her students. If you are a teacher, reflect on a time when you have faced a similar situation and describe how you would have handled it, given the context of your school and your students. What went well, and what would you do differently next time? If you are not a teacher, relax, as you already know that you would have done a better job.

Comparative task

Compare this text to an online newspaper article about Australian teachers (select one which includes the reader comments immediately after the article). Draw up a table in your exercise book or on your computer to list the differences. The table below provides an example to get you started. Try to find at least five further differences.

Semi-Educated	*Newspaper articles and reader comments*
Presents teachers as hard-working and self-sacrificing	Presents teachers as stupid and lazy

Further activities

There are many excellent memoirs, novels, movies and television shows about teachers. If you are not sick to death of teachers whingeing at you then you might like to spend some more time investigating these and compiling a list of reasons why you enjoyed them more than *Semi-Educated*. You could create a webpage, a blog, a book review or even a TikTok to record your findings. Remember to mention the name of the text, the date it was published and the author's name.

Special credit from Mrs Brooks and Bad Apple Press

If you think you can do so without too much inner conflict or self-deception, tell a friend that you enjoyed *Semi-Educated* or write a positive review of it somewhere public. Small Australian publishers rely heavily on favourable word of mouth. If you loathed the book or if you think a two-star review is positive, please tell an enemy that you loved this book.